THE NEW ECONOMIC HISTORY OF THE RAILWAYS

The New Economic History of the Railways

PATRICK O'BRIEN

CROOM HELM LONDON

© 1977 Patrick O'Brien
Croom Helm Ltd, 2-10 St John's Road, London SW11

British Library Cataloguing in Publication Data

O'Brien, Patrick
    The new economic history of the railways
    1. Railroads – History
    I. Title
    385'. 1'09   HE1021

    ISBN 0-85664-531-1

Printed in Great Britain by offset lithography by
Billing & Sons Ltd, Guildford, London and Worcester

CONTENTS

TABLES AND DIAGRAMS

For H.J.H. and R.M.H.

INTRODUCTION

New economic history is characterised by rigorous specification of hypothesis and by the deployment of economic theory and quantitative techniques, which, its practitioners claim, should solve many of the problems less carefully defined and more circumspectly answered by older historical methods. The new discipline's most famous departures from tradition have produced unorthodox conclusions on slavery in the Southern States of America and about railroads in Britain, Russia and the United States. Thus Fogel and Engerman found southern slave agriculture to be '35 per cent more efficient than the northern system of family farming' and, again by measurement, discovered 'the material (not psychological) conditions of the lives of slaves compared favourably with those of free industrial workers'. In their equally famous but less dramatic investigations into the impact of railways on the economies of America, Britain, Russia and elsewhere, new economic historians offer statistical indicators of that impact which, *prima facie*, controvert received wisdom, which saw railways as an important and sometimes vital ingredient of economic growth in Europe and America over the second half of the nineteenth century.

Neither of these interpretations has passed unchallenged. The new economic history of slavery and railroads has generated a rich controversy, and, as Trevor-Roper aptly put it, 'history without controversy is not history'. Nevertheless, it remains difficult for students of history and of economic history not only to keep pace with the literature but also to comprehend the dimensions and elements of a debate which ranges across several countries and at least four academic disciplines – history, economics, statistics and philosophy.

This book was designed to help those interested both in new economic history and the history of railways to appreciate its major findings and to understand the strengths and weaknesses of economic theory and quantitative techniques applied to grand historical themes. The book is a text, offered as a work of exposition and criticism. It aims to tell students (particularly those less conversant with economics and statistics) what has been said and what has and has not been demonstrated by the new economic history of railways.

Textbooks are not original. They rest heavily (as the bibliography acknowledges) upon the works of other scholars – in this case and to a great extent upon the original researches of Fishlow, Fogel, Hawke, Metzer, Fenoaltea and their critics into the role of railways in the economic development of the United States, Britain, Russia and Italy. The debate stimulated by their findings is not only about the history of transport but is also directly concerned with fact and method in economic history. For those who study the history of modern economic growth and for those who prefer to reflect about historical method in relation to concrete historical issues, the new economic history of railways is one of the most intellectually exciting and important controversies in the subject.

My conclusions come at the end of the book, but if I finally conclude that new economic history has emphatically not offered a definite solution to the impact of railways upon economic growth in America, Russia, Britain and Italy this does not imply that attempts to specify and to measure that impact are not works of scholarship which must be taken seriously by the discipline. To read and engage in debates of this quality should, I believe, form part of the education of students in economic history and in history. If this text prompts students to read and reflect more efficiently upon the literature listed in the bibliography it will have achieved its limited purpose.

The arrangement of the text is comparative and analytical. Comparisons of the contribution of railways across several countries should bring out differences in method among new economic historians and highlight contrasts in the significance of railways between settled and mature economies such as Britain and Italy and 'frontier societies' like the United States as well as countries such as Russia and Mexico, where railways helped to surmount bottlenecks to economic growth posed by a terrain hostile to the movement of freight and people. Such studies also contribute evidence to the wider discussion on the role of social overhead capital and externalities in economic development.

The format of the book is first to contrast new and older approaches to the history of transport in Chapter 1. This chapter will then be followed by two chapters which are a critical exposition of the methods used to quantify the contribution of railways to economic growth by means of counterfactual speculation and the measurement of social savings. A survey and appraisal of the data used in these exercises is set out as an appendix at the end of the book. Chapter 4 discusses the empirical and conceptual difficulties involved in the attempts to quantify the impact of railways by an alternative index, namely the social rate of return on the capital invested for the construction and diffusion of railways. Chapters 5 and 6 are concerned with the effect of railways on the rest of the economy that flowed (a) from expenditures by railway companies on labour, capital goods, and industrial inputs, and (b) from market integration, access to natural resources and the relocation of economic activity, which followed from the diffusion of railways.

Friends and colleagues have been more than helpful. Detailed and critical comments upon an earlier draft of this text by Stan Engerman, Al Fishlow, Bob Gallman, Max Hartwell, Gary Hawke, Jenny Phillips and Colin White have clarified and improved the argument at many points. Elizabeth Stevens coped cheerfully and efficiently in typing my scrody drafts. My wife deserves special thanks for help with the index. Unfortunately, I alone am responsible for the errors and omissions that undoubtedly remain in the printed version.

1 NEW AND OLDER APPROACHES TO ECONOMIC HISTORY

1 New Economic History

A general context for the academic study of economic history can be found in a contemporary problem — the distribution of wealth and income among nations of the world. Since most of this observed inequality has arisen because economic growth in a small group of countries in Western Europe, North America and Australasia proceeded more rapidly than elsewhere in the world, new and old economic history are part of an enquiry into why national output increased faster in some countries and regions than others.

To organise their research and answers to this question most economic historians employ a conceptual framework derived ultimately from neo-classical economics. Thus many of the monographs and texts published in recent years are cast in the framework of a production function. New economic historians employ this form more explicitly and rigorously than their predecessors. Production function analysis has given rise to sophisticated studies in econometrics but its underlying logic is simple enough. Final goods and services produced by an economy (or region, or any part of an economy) emanate from inputs. In theory inputs include everything put into the process of production. For output to increase (or its rate of growth to accelerate) either more inputs or inputs of better quality are required. In other words, higher growth rates might come either from more land, labour, capital, education and organisation of the same kind, or from improvements to the quality of one or any bundle of inputs employed to produce output.

Old economic history described how inputs and technical change interacted to produce, for example, the acceleration of national output in Britain in the late eighteenth century or a similar change in Belgium, France, Germany and America decades later. From such books as Ashton's *Industrial Revolution,* Henri See's *Histoire Économique de la France,* Werner Sombart's *Die Deutsche Volkwirtschaft,* or Faulkner's *American Economic History,* students learned to appreciate how and where different elements fitted into American, British, French or German economic development in the eighteenth and nineteenth centuries. The final conclusions offered by older economic historians

tended to be as cautious as those published by their colleagues in
general history to explain the great discontinuities of domestic politics
of international relations. Thus as they understood it, economic development came from a multiplicity of inputs, interacting with technical and
institutional change, and contributing with different intensity to the
upward momentum of an economy over the long run.

New economic history regarded this kind of conclusion as sympto-
matic of a failure to exploit the potentialities of economics and
econometrics. Economics, they held, could assist economic historians
to specify rigorously the mechanism through which any selected input
operated upon the growth of the economy, while econometrics,
particularly multiple regression analysis, could help them to quantify
the contribution of each and, if possible, every input relevant to
economic progress.

Inevitably the larger volume of publications by economists on the
dynamics of growth influenced economic history and deepened
understanding of the process or mechanisms of past development.
Such comprehension seems, however, to have increased continuously
generation after generation, and, if anything is really new, it resides
less in the exploitation of recent discoveries in economic theory, and
rather more in the conscious and sophisticated efforts at quantification.
Perhaps the signal distinction between traditional and modern
approaches to the subject consists in a sustained effort to measure
the importance of inputs selected for study. Whether the subject in
question is the effects of the Navigation Acts, profits from the slave
trade, or the closure of the Second Bank of the United States, new
economic history will include an attempt to quantify its contribution
to national output and the growth rate.

At a macro level the emphasis on quantification attracted interest
in long run production functions, or growth accountancy, which
purports to separate out and to measure the contribution made to
increased output from different inputs. The results of these studies
(for several years under attack on conceptual as well as more obvious
empirical grounds) suggest that the development of the now affluent
nations, at least during the twentieth century, emanated not from
changes in the quantities of capital and labour employed in production
but came instead (to an overwhelming degree) from a 'residual' loosely
referred to as technical progress — a heading which includes new
knowledge, more efficient forms of productive organisation and
improvements in the health, education and motivation of the labour
force. Economic historians now recognise that the stress given to

technical progress for the modern period, and by some older economic historians for the Industrial Revolution, may not apply to the eighteenth and nineteenth centuries and in any case the magnitude of this 'residual' or the share of a nation's growth unexplained by additions to the quantity of capital and labour employed by an economy seems to be a 'coefficient of ignorance' perhaps nearly as great as that implicit in the cautious general conclusions offered in historical texts, written two or three decades ago.

New economic history can certainly be distinguished by its greater emphasis on quantification, and the majority of its more convincing contributions might be divided into two categories. Either the book or article takes the form of an original and theoretically refined statistical series for national or regional income, levels of investment in education, internal migration, a dollar sterling exchange rate, inter-regional mortgage and interest rates, and so on. Alternatively, new economic historians have supplied answers to the kind of circumscribed questions where the tools of economic theory in general and neo-classical analysis in particular can be used with maximum effect.

For example, they have been successful in specifying and measuring sources of productivity change in several industries, including grain and dairy farming, shipping and shipbuilding, railways, iron and cotton textiles. Their explanations for the diffusion of innovations across industries and regions are also impressive, and their assessment of the impact of the State in such fields as banking regulation, tariffs, federal land law displays a comprehension of economic theory well beyond anything found in general history.

As history, new economic history is logically rigorous and technically sophisticated. With the help from computers and other mechanical aids, it has generated impressive and useful amounts of data and offers quantified answers to a whole range of questions that can be posed about the development of firms and industries, as well as the economic impact of circumscribed institutional changes. The new approach has demonstrated a capacity to deal with economic growth at the micro level. But less success, and certainly more controversy, has attended its efforts to go beyond firms, industries and particular institutions in order to deal with the grand themes of economic history played out at the level of national or regional development.

For example, few historians accept the studies of the impact of war upon economic development in Britain and the United States or the role of property rights in the rise of the Western World as more than preliminary and rather theoretical forays into complex problems. Furthermore, although ingenious suggestions that the late Victorian economy grew at something like a warranted rate challenges the orthodoxy of a British climacteric and will certainly engender useful debate, neither theory nor statistics are likely to resolve disputes about a reasonable or plausible rate of structural change. Similarly, historians may now be tempted to conclude that the efficiency of slavery and its impact upon the growth of the Southern States in America is probably in the end not reducible to testable propositions that can be conceptualised and weighted within the framework of neo-classical economics.

2 The Older Economic History of Railways

Perhaps it is true to say that new economic history entered a state of 'take-off' with the appearance of famous and controversial attempts to assess the contribution of railways to economic progress in the nineteenth century. A pioneer article by Fogel on the United States appeared in 1962 and was followed by books from Fogel and Fishlow in 1965. This intellectual innovation inspired research on British, Russian, Italian and other national railways. Since railways have long been considered among the most important, if not *the* most important of all the inventions made available to producers in the nineteenth century, an outline and critique of the methods employed to quantify the effects of railways on national economic development should bring out the conceptual and statistical difficulties involved when new economic historians tackle the grand themes of history.

Before passing on to an analysis of these new methods and conclusions it may be germane to point out that older economic histories of transport not only supplied historical detail, they helped students to understand the revolution in transport in the eighteenth and nineteenth centuries and they also outlined the ways or mechanisms through which improved forms of transport effected economic development in Britain, America, Russia and elsewhere.
Thus from the writings of such historians as Jackman, Willan and Lewin on Britain, Jenks, Hunter and Goodrich on the United States and Ames, Westwood and Blackwell on Russia it is possible to derive the following outline of the nature of the transport revolution as well as some perception of the main functional relationships between technological progress in transport and economic growth.

Traditional transport systems employed wind and animal power to move freight on rivers, lakes and seas, and along natural or surfaced terrain. For heavy and bulky commodities, transport by water was normally cheaper and quicker than movement overland. Nineteenth-century industrialisation was accompanied by the diffusion of better methods of transport which consisted of roads with improved surfaces, artificial waterways, railed ways and the application of steam power to carriers by rail and water. These innovations (which might be described as part of a long-term technological shift within the transport system from natural forms of propulsion and natural routes to mechanical means of propulsion and man-made ways) reduced the costs of moving goods across space and time. Such reductions could be particularly significant for commodities that were bulky or heavy in relation to value (for example, bricks, minerals, grains, timber and metallurgical products) and also for perishable goods where speed of delivery was vital.

Freight costs declined not only because the volume of real resources (manpower, animals, animal feedstuffs, land, timber and other industrial inputs) required to transport a ton of commodities over a given distance decreased, but also because innovations like steam propulsion meant that commodities could be transhipped with far greater speed and continuity, which implied a greater utilisation of the capacity employed in transportation. For transport users the increased speed, regularity and reliability of delivery reduced losses on goods in transit and obviated the need to hold large stocks of finished or intermediate goods as a precaution against irregular or slow deliveries. Thus as their storage and inventory charges per unit of output declined, producers could transfer investible funds from circulating to fixed capital.

Above all, more efficient transport technology reduced the costs of fuel, raw materials and construction materials to industry and agriculture and enabled industrialists and farmers to sell their products to consumers at lower prices. Such innovations extended the market in the sense that they opened up new sources of supply for raw materials and other inputs and permitted producers to sell more cheaply over a wider area. Thus for agriculture cheaper transport made it possible for farmers to purchase a larger volume of bulky inputs like natural fertilisers, bricks, clay, timber and other building materials. The share of farm output marketed on larger and more stable markets expanded while the commercialisation of agriculture encouraged farmers to innovate and specialise. For industry, input prices also fell and wider markets permitted enterprises to exploit economies of scale and specialisation. For both sectors more efficient transport helped to break down geographical and social barriers to competition. Competition in turn assisted in the diffusion of improved technology and pushed producers towards higher levels of efficiency. Innovations in transport prompted firms to take greater advantage of economies attendant upon regional and international specialisation. Location patterns ceased to be determined exclusively in terms of proximity to markets and producers found it possible to locate their enterprises closer to supplies of cheaper natural resources, raw materials or to labour.

Furthermore, the improved transport systems themselves also widened markets because they made direct demands for inputs upon several other industries and induced expansion and possibly technical progress in those industries. Deliveries of constructional materials, coal, iron and engineering products to a growing transport sector could stimulate the adoption of new techniques of production and could lead to economies of scale in several industries supplying intermediate goods to that sector.

Finally the development and diffusion of new transport technology engendered a range of spin-offs that provided economic benefits for the economy as a whole over and above the advantages derived by agricultural and industrial producers from the availability of cheaper transport. For example, labour became more mobile. Part of the technology designed for the transport of freight and passengers could be adapted for alternative uses elsewhere in an economy. Again, the training of managerial and skilled labour either directly in transport enterprises or by firms which supplied inputs to the transport sector increased the supply of skilled manpower. New transport systems also made voracious demands for funds which brought about improvements to the institutions and techniques of the capital market, which not only rendered investible funds more mobile but may have added to the supply of foreign and domestic savings available for investment.

This brief summary of the functions of transport in nineteenth-century industrialisation omits all historical detail and concentrates upon connections between canals and railways on the one hand and the rest of the economy on the other. These interrelationships are contained, in more or less explicit form, in most economic histories of transport written before the 1960s and their restatement should enable us to go on to analyse and appraise the original contribution of the new economic history of railways which is, as the first part of the chapter suggested, concerned, above all, to quantify the influence of railways on economic progress.

2 SOCIAL SAVINGS, COUNTERFACTUALS AND SOCIAL RATES OF RETURN

1 Initial Definitions

Railways came late in the process of improvement to the transport systems of Europe and America. To many contemporaries and to some historians the far greater speed and regularity of movement by rail represented a great discontinuity in the development of transport and for that reason they were disposed to exaggerate their impact upon economic and social change in general. But it is fair to suggest that many histories of transport are overwhelmingly (perhaps tediously) descriptive and do not commit themselves one way or the other on the effects of railways.

For new economic historians the influence of railways upon the long-term growth of any economy can only be properly assessed by measuring reductions in the cost of sending freight by rail compared to alternative forms of transport. They then go on to evaluate the extent to which such reductions in the costs of transporting agricultural and industrial products widened markets and thereby promoted economies associated with larger scale enterprise, specialisation, increased competition, more efficient patterns of location and other economies in real resources, often loosely specified in older economic histories of transport but which are derived ultimately from Adam Smith's observations in *The Wealth of Nations*.

For new economic history a full enquiry into the impact of railways also includes an evaluation of the effects of 'feedbacks' from railways upon those industries that supplied inputs to the new transport system as well as an attempt to measure the effect of railways upon supplies of capital, skilled labour and new techniques of production, compared to alternative forms of transport. Railways seldom initiated tendencies connected with the widening of markets or the saving of real resources, but they carried forward such tendencies. The problem for new economic historians was to specify and measure with what effect or by how much?

To help them evaluate the particular contribution made by railways to economic progress in the nineteenth century, new economic historians make use of three constructs: counterfactuals, social savings and the social rate of return on investment. At this point it will help the exposition if we define each construct in a simple and preliminary way and postpone refinement until students grasp the essential ideas underlying each concept and can appreciate the way they have been deployed in the new economic history of railways.

A social rate of return is a standard concept in the economics of investment appraisal. It is designed to measure the gains or benefits that might or has accrued to society as a whole from the investment of a given amount of capital in a particular project.

Counterfactual propositions are implicit in all historical arguments of the kind which says A was an important (or even an insignificant) cause of B. In making such causal statements historians have in mind the difference that any factor A made to the outcome of an event B and that is the same as comparing the situation with and without B. For example, the assertion that the poor quality of French entrepreneurs retarded economic growth in France implies that had the French economy been managed by some alternative business élite, its growth rate would have been more impressive. The basic difficulty with all counterfactual arguments is that they are based upon historical situations that never pertained, and there is no logical way of deciding if conclusions drawn from such methods are correct or even plausible. While almost any historical statement which seeks to weigh the relative importance of causal factors contains an implicit counterfactual, as a heuristic device it can only be persuasively employed where a plausible alternative can be properly specified. For historians this rules out the use of counterfactuals in fruitless but enjoyable discussions of Russia without the Revolution or Napoleon victorious at Waterloo. New economic historians, confronted with a historiography that made large claims for the impact of railways on material development in the nineteenth century, made full use of economic theory to assist them to describe a counterfactual economy without railways and have attempted to quantify the difference in levels of national output realised by the actual economies of America, Russia and Britain with railways and hypothetical alternatives deprived of the services of railways.

Social savings is more difficult to define in simple language and there are differences in the content of the construct as used by Fogel and other new economic historians of railways; differences which turn largely upon the *ceteris paribus* conditions deemed to pertain in the counterfactual economy deprived of railways. For expository purposes such complexities will, however, be ignored at this point and will be considered in Chapter 3.

Meanwhile social savings might be defined initially as the loss impos-

ed upon an economy through the abrupt closure of its most efficient mode of transport several decades after the construction of railways first commenced. This loss can, in principle, be measured provided :
(a)   The historian can estimate the services performed for the economy by its railway system, as conventionally measured in physical units of ton miles of freight carried on trains over one year.
(b)   The historian assumes that, when deprived of the services of railways, enterprises continued to ship the same volume and composition of freight previously carried on trains by the cheapest feasible combination of waggons and boats. In economists' terms the price elasticity of demand for transport is assumed to be low.

In a competitive economy the transfer of millions of ton miles of freight from railways to less efficient forms of transport was bound to be more expensive because: (i) costs per ton mile by the substitute combination of boat and waggon would exceed costs by rail; (ii) freight would be forced to travel extra miles along roads and waterways compared to the actual and more direct routes it travelled by rail; (iii) it was normally quicker and less risky to despatch freight by railways than by boat and waggon.
(c)   Thus historians must also estimate the extra distance travelled by freight along roads and waterways; the extra charge collected by hauliers from producers when they despatched freight by boat and waggon; the additional costs borne by enterprises as a result of the extra time taken as well as the losses sustained by sending freight by boat and waggon instead of by train.

Given the availability of data, or rather the possibility of estimation, social savings (defined in this preliminary way) can then be measured as the sum of all additional charges incurred by enterprises to transport commodities by ship and waggon. Social savings is then defined as equal to the extra benefit obtained by society from the normal operation of its railway system or the costs to society from its failure to operate over one year, while the volume and pattern of freight shipments remained constant.

Fogel did not offer an estimate for social savings as defined in this preliminary way. But Fishlow, Hawke and Metzer all employed the same counterfactual (an economy deprived of the services of railways for one year) and calculated the aggregate cost of transferring the actual volume of commodities moved by rail onto ships and waggons for transhipment between the same points of production and distribution. Fishlow's estimate for social savings for America in 1859 comes to about $134 million.

For England and Wales Hawke put the total additional cost of re-allocation in 1865 at around £28 million. According to Metzer the social saving which the Russian economy and society derived from its railway network can be estimated at 890 million roubles: 'This was the value of the resources saved by having railroads operate and ship about 60% of Russian freight in 1907.'

It will immediately occur to historians of America, Britain and Russia that the task of collecting, processing and validating the data required to produce even rough estimates of social savings for any year in the nineteenth century poses formidable problems. They will certainly and properly wish to be satisfied that the evidential basis for such an exercise is reasonably secure. Detailed verification of the evidence presented has been undertaken in Appendix 1.

At this point it should suffice to summarise the conclusions which seem to flow from a survey of data. Statistics for the nineteenth century are always hard to find. All historians will be grateful for the substantial amounts of new information generated by these exercises in quantitative history. It is, moreover, proper to admit that other people's data are often scrutinised in a more exacting way than one's own. But historians of all persuasions are all taught one big thing – facts are important. While the quality of the evidence used to support the estimates of social savings contained in the new economic history of railways obviously varies from study to study, it appears, in general terms, to be vulnerable on two counts: (a) the facts for output (ton miles) of freight transhipped between producers and consumers in the counterfactual economy deprived of railways seem less than satisfactory for the calculation of social savings; (b) the range of data employed to measure the charges (prices) by hauliers of freight by road and water, particularly the former, seems to be thin and possibly unrepresentative.

Historians interested in the evidence should turn to Appendix 1. This exposition will, however, proceed to analyse the meaning and inferences that might be drawn from estimates of social saving for Britain, America and Russia as defined above.

2 Social Savings as a Ratio of Gross National Product

Absolute totals in dollars, sterling or roubles tell us very little and economic historians invariably express their statistics as relatives in order to convey perceptible information. Gross national product which is the aggregate measure of output produced by a country over one year seems an obvious denominator for estimates of social savings.

For 1859 Fishlow adopted the 'not unreasonable' assumption of
unitary elasticity of demand for transport services and put social savings
on freight alone at about 3.3 per cent of gross national product.
Hawke's estimate for England and Wales in 1865 is around 4 per cent
of national income. Metzer expressed the share of 'freight social savings'
in Russian GNP for 1907 at about 4.6 per cent. Fogel's estimate for
social savings which accrued to the American economy in 1890 from
the operation of railroads is defined differently but comes to 4.7 per
cent of social output.

To historians accustomed to reading (perhaps even to writing)
eulogies on the contribution of railways to economic progress in
the nineteenth century the percentages will appear on the low side.
But that is the inevitable result of dividing small by far larger
numbers. The significance of any input defined for study can be
made to seem small by expressing its contribution to output as
share of a national aggregate. Such results tell us that the national
output for any selected year would probably not decline by many
percentage points if the economy suffered from the closure of its
canals, cotton factories, steel mills, coal mines, technical schools,
banks or from any other sub-sector of industry, agriculture,
transport and services. Providing substitutes exist, no single part of the
productive system is very important.

New economic historians remind us that this sort of ratio is a
simple test of the axiom that railways formed an *indispensable*
ingredient in American economic progress. Chapter 1 of Fogel's
Railroads and American Economic Growth certainly supports
that contention. Yet some historians now ask if that axiom ever
constituted a serious plank of historiography. Fogel's quotations
merely demonstrate that Americans, from the editor of *The
Toledo Blade* in 1847 through to Professor Bolino in 1961, tended
to write in hyperbolic terms about the beneficient effects of their
railroads. More serious scholars of the transport system — like
Carter Goodrich — displayed no taste for superlatives. We should
concede, however, it is helpful to juxtapose the real costs of
closing down railways against the more flowery adjectives employed
to describe their role in British, Russian and American history, and
the calculation of social saving serves to warn historians that words
like crucial, vital, decisive and revolutionary could and probably
should be confronted with percentages. These ratios are also usefully
employed to make scholarly points to the effect that 'no single
innovation was vital for economic growth in the nineteenth century'

and (to quote Fogel's conclusions again) 'while cheap inland transportation was a necessary condition for economic growth, satisfaction
of this condition did not entail a specific form of transportation'.
Such statements eloquently argued and backed by evidence are well
directed at Rostovian notions of 'leading sectors' and 'take offs';
perhaps also at some of Schumpeter's more incautious remarks on
the dramatic impact of certain nineteenth-century innovations. Thus
the ratios find their place in debates about the origins of economic
growth in nineteenth-century Europe and America and in the more
amorphous debate of balanced and unbalanced growth.

Fishlow and Hawke were not concerned to refute 'axioms of
indispensability' which could hardly be proclaimed for America's
railroads in 1859 or for the role of railways in British economic
development. Metzer recognised that 'in general, it is quite difficult
to determine whether a given quality is absolutely big or small'.
Fishlow judged his estimate of social saving to be 'an impressive
contribution' and was properly concerned about the real meaning
that could be attached to 'such a simple ratio'. It would certainly
not be difficult to conceive of ways of making the absolute level
of social saving attributed to railways appear more important. For
example, since these studies are essentially investigations into the
relationship between railways and economic growth, estimates of
the losses imposed upon an economy by the closure of railways
could be expressed as percentages of the trend rate of growth of
national product, an exercise which produced ratios of 60 per cent
for America in 1859, 164 per cent for Britain in 1865, 104 per
cent for United States in 1890 and just over 200 per cent of the
trend rate of growth for total output observed in Russia between
1883 and 1913.

In other words, once social savings are considered in a dynamic
context of long-term growth, the focus of attention shifts logically
to the compensation required for the loss of output imposed on a
country by a shut-down of its railways over one year. There are
several ways of appreciating this point but the addition to the long-
term growth rate required in order to replace the income or output
lost by society while its trains ceased to operate seems relevant.
Of course, the answer depends upon the rate of growth and the time
scale selected for replacement. Some notion of the degree of effort
involved can, however, be obtained from British and American data
by assuming that both societies opted to replace the real output lost
through the closure of railways in 1865 and 1890 over a five year period.

The trend growth rate for the British economy (1841-51 to 1871-81) amounted to 2.5 per cent a year. To make up for the hypothetical loss of income suffered from the closure of railways in 1865 over the five year period 1865-70 would mean raising the growth rate to nearly 3.5 per cent — that is by about 40 per cent. With a capital output ratio (estimated by the Deane and Cole at about 4), the funds required to compensate for closure would imply an increase of 40 per cent per annum in the gross investment rate and a cut of 5 per cent a year in consumer expenditure.

For America the economy grew at an average rate of about 4½ per cent a year, 1874-83 to 1894-93, and to make up the loss suffered from the shut down of railways in 1890 over the subsequent five years would require a sudden jump of 22 per cent in the growth rate of gross national product, an increase from around 24 per cent to nearly 29 per cent in the gross investment rate and a cut of 7 per cent in total consumption in order to provide the investible funds required for additional capital formation.

Economists know the difficulties of increasing secular growth rates by one or two percentage points over the short run, and the illustrative detail set out above provides a realistic interpretation of the changes in rates of investment and cuts in consumption that would be required over a five year period to make up for the hypothetical shut down of railways in 1865 or 1890. No doubt other and equally valid ways could be devised for comprehending the impact of depriving the American or British economies of railways. For example, one possible alternative would be to calculate the additional inflows of foreign loans required in order to keep consumption at the levels sustained with the aid of railways.

Hawke argued that social savings is a useful indication of 'how great was the impact of railways as an example of technical change . . . when the impact of technical change is defined as the cost of replacing the particular development in a given year'. Of course this formulation begs the question of whether the significance of an innovation can be appreciated or perceived if impact is defined in that way and it also leaves open the choice of an appropriate standard for comparison. If historians chose to evaluate the influence of an innovation in terms of the cost of its removal then the impact of railways needs to be compared with the effects of other innovations. If a selection of nineteenth-century innovations could be ranked in terms of their individual effect upon the level of national product at points in time when that contribution reached its maximum level, then economists could perhaps compare the measured impact of railways with, say, canals; puddled iron with steel and steam power with electricity. At present such ratios are not available and until they are no firm basis exists for a proper assessment of the relative importance of railways.

Even if we take such a suggestion as an agenda for research, the comparability of different innovations comes immediately into question. The comparisons set out above seem sensible enough. But as Fishlow observed, 'with unlimited inputs of resources any activity might claim a large effect upon total income'. In other words the investible funds required for the introduction and spread of innovations throughout an economy varied considerably from case to case. Thus there may be no substitute for calculating the social rate of return on capital invested.

Finally, the whole exercise raises apparently insoluble difficulties of defining an innovation and comparing its impact with others of a similar nature and cost. On the issue of definition it seems just as reasonable to define innovation in transport in the nineteenth century as the application of steam propulsion to carriers on railed-ways and waterways, but to calculate the real cost to an economy of depriving its transport system of steam power would be a mammoth undertaking. One would guess, however, that there could be little debate about the significance of social savings from an innovation widely defined as steam power employed in transport.

3 Social Savings for One Year?

Serious questions also arise about inference from statistics related to a single year. Fogel argued:

> The answer depends on the relative efficiency of the railroad in 1890 as compared with earlier periods. If the railroad was relatively more efficient in 1890 than in any previous year, the social saving per unit of transportation in 1890 would have exceeded the saving per unit in all previous years. The available evidence suggests that this was indeed the case.

Fishlow is more sceptical and regards 'a single year chosen at the end of the period as failing to convey accurately the character of the contribution over the entire thirty odd years railroad services were available'. Hawke makes no explicit claim that the ratio he presents for 1865 is (like Fogel's) an upper bound estimate of social saving for all previous years but he does expect 'in a growing economy the absolute value of social saving to increase monotonically, except perhaps for cyclical fluctuations'.

Monotonically means with consistent movement in one direction. Neither Fogel or Hawke would argue that the economic gains from railways increased along some discernable and smooth trend, although Hawke's tabulations for years before 1865 appear to give that impression. When Fishlow extrapolated his result backwards he found that the benefits from railroads fell from $156 million to $79 million in just five years. Moreover, gains from investment in social overhead capital tends to be bunched in years that succeed relatively long periods of gestation with great cyclical variation over time in capital output ratios.

Inference is always difficult and good economists like Fishlow, Fogel, Hawke and Metzer will avoid such obvious pitfalls as years of cyclical downturn and unemployment. Fishlow's backward extrapolation does indicate, however, that inference about the *extent* of social saving for the period preceding that year selected for measurement is impossible to make because even if the long-term direction of change is upward, the social savings from railways might vary widely in the short run.

Finally, to look forward as well as backward, the selection of years beyond 1859, 1865, 1890 and 1907 could produce far higher ratios of social saving to national product, at least up to the period when automobiles became a serious competitor to railways. When Hawke extrapolated his 'preliminary' estimate of social savings forward from 1865 to 1890 (in order to analyse the productivity of investment in railroads) he, nevertheless, found that its share in the national income of the United Kingdom more than doubled — from 1.7 per cent to 4.7 per cent. Hawke's data also show that the ratio of total social savings to the national income of England and Wales went up from 4.1 per cent in 1865 to over 11 per cent in 1890. Fogel delineated his interest as the half-century preceding the year selected for measurement, but this did not preclude Hacker from making the germane observation that ten years is a long time in American economic history. Hacker's assertion is that by 1900 the locus of production for wheat and beef had shifted further westward onto lands where 'water transportation (even including the building of the canals projected by Fogel) would have been well nigh impossible'.

When divergent views of the importance of railroads can be obtained from the vantage point of different years, historians should think carefully about the temporal relevance of generalisation based on calculations for any single year.

3 SOCIAL SAVINGS AND ASSOCIATED COUNTERFACTUALS IN THE CONTEXT OF ECONOMIC GROWTH

1 Some Definitions of Social Savings Again

Let us begin by looking again at the definitions of social savings offered in the new economic history of railways and the kind of counter-factual economies implied by their deployment in exercises in quantitative history. A clear preliminary definition is where 'social savings in any given year is . . . the difference between the actual cost of shipping goods in that year with the alternative cost of shipping exactly the same goods between the same points without railroads'. Fishlow's concept is designed to

> take explicit account of the amount of cost reduction involved, not only its existence. Aggregated over the entire railroad system this provides a measure of the financial savings shippers enjoyed from the innovation, and, from a social viewpoint, some notion of the reduction in resource inputs required for transportation.

For Hawke social saving is

> the cost of replacing the particular development in a given year or the percentage of national income that would have to be rediverted to sustain the economy without an innovation at the level it actually reached with that innovation.

Metzer's formulation expresses social savings in terms of 'the additional real cost that the economy would bear in shipping the railroads volume of freight (without changing patterns of shipments) by the best alternative modes. This is obviously an upper bound of the true social saving since quantities are not allowed to adjust to changes in transport cost that would result from this shift.'

The related counterfactual is an economy prevented from using its railway system for exactly one year during which time everything else remained exactly as it would have been with the railways. Fishlow, Hawke and Metzer calculate consistently in terms of their definitions and associated counterfactuals which (data problems apart) were designed to measure the 'transport savings railroads provided as a historical fact'. Fishlow used social savings primarily to help him measure the rate of return on capital invested in railroads. If carefully handled, Hawke regards his estimate as useful and un-ambiguous information about the impact of railways, as an example of technical change. Metzer expected that the significance of his estimate for Russia 'lies primarily in translating a major part of the qualitative assertions regarding the railroads role in Russian economic development into orders of magnitude' . . . which could 'at least cast some doubt on postulates of single determinants of growth'.

There is no harm repeating a point made earlier that the difficulty with counterfactual speculation in economic history is that counter-factual economies cannot be realised or specified in terms that can be verified. By including the phrase *ceteris paribus* in their definitions of social savings, Fishlow, Hawke and Metzer explicitly excluded any adjustments of a positive or negative kind to the closure of railways. Historians may or may not accept their specification of the American economy in 1859, the British economy in 1865 or the Russian economy in 1907 as economies that would have remain-ed exactly the same, deprived of the services of railways for one year. Alternatively they may well regard the *ceteris paribus* condition as a plausible and useful heuristic device to employ when measuring the impact of closing down the railways for a period as short as one year.

Fogel was not, however, content with such a restricted definition of social savings and he preferred to conduct his calculations within the ambit of an alternative version of social savings to the one cited in Chapter 2. His revised and preferred concept is designed to specify an upper bound or maximal level for social savings where

> social savings . . . is the difference between the actual level of national income in 1890 and the level of national income that would have prevailed *if the economy had made the most efficient possible transport adjustment to the absence of the . . . railroad.*

In other words, Fogel dispensed with the *ceteris paribus* condition adopted by other new economic historians and allowed his counter-factual economy to adjust to the closure of railroads in 1890. His postulated adjustments are confined to agriculture and the transport sector. Fogel observed, quite plausibly, that the area of land farmed in America in 1890 would have been diminished without the railroad and in the counterfactual economy he shifted the hypothetical margin of cultivation closer to navigable waterways. He also expected (quite plausibly) that if the Americans had been deprived of railroads they would have added to the canal system and improved public roads. In his counterfactual economy the canal system was extended 5,000 miles and the roads made more efficient in order to cope with the freight shifted off the railroads. It is interesting to observe that these adjustments cut social savings in 1890 from nearly 9 per cent of gross national product (calculated from Fogel's data on a *ceteris paribus* assumption) to 4.7 per cent as estimated by Fogel to allow for the range of technical adaptation outlined above.

Fogel's hypothetical economy is given resources and time to adjust to the closure of railroads. Total output (or more specifically agricultural output) and freight transported is allowed to fall. But the range of feasible adjustments allowed for is limited and we are not offered any detailed defence of this particular counterfactual. If the economy is given time to compensate for the shut-down of railroads, presumably the closure envisaged is for more than one year and in that case the patterns of substitution and response that might have occurred in the American economy seems arbitrarily restricted. Again we are reminded of the basic logical difficulty inherent in this kind of speculation — how is the verification to be conducted? Presumably the answer could run in terms of economic theories related to the growth and development of market economies. But is growth theory strong enough to bear the weight of counterfactual speculation which is logically compelled to range across the whole economy?

Thus Fogel's definition of social saving falls between the *ceteris paribus* assumption employed by Hawke, Fishlow and Metzer and the kind of counterfactual required to measure the contribution of railroads to the observed rate of economic growth achieved by different countries over the nineteenth century. It is a heroic and instructive attempt to escape, without loss of rigour, from the confines of the partial equilibrium framework taken over from economic theory into historical analysis. With all the daring of an innovator, Fogel broke the intellectual bonds that confine all economic historians who wish to say something definite about one of the major sources of economic growth. But if economic historians hope to measure the effect of an innovation on long-term development, social savings must be redefined to include the total range of influences exercised by that innovation upon the economy at large. The associated counterfactual would *not* then be an economy compelled to operate without railways for a single year, but rather a hypothetical economy which derived absolutely no benefits at all from railways because they were simply never constructed in Britain, America, or Russia. Theoretically the historian would then compare not just social savings achieved by railways over rival forms of transport for any selected year but also the total contribution to national output obtained from the construction and operation of railways up to a given point in time. Such a definition of social savings provides for a radical departure from assumptions holding other things equal embodied in the definitions employed by Metzer, Hawke and Fishlow and partially relaxed by Fogel when he allowed for shifts in the margin of cultivation and the construction of canals and improvement to roads. Historical exercises of this kind have not and probably cannot be attempted. A retrodictive cost benefit analysis seems in many ways even more difficult than the normal predictive analysis. Meanwhile we agree with Hawke's statement that 'social savings does not describe chronologically all the changes in the economy that resulted from the introduction of railways'. In fact Hawke explicitly eschewed any attempt 'to describe the differences between the economy that actually existed in 1865 and what the economy would have been like had railways not been introduced'.

2 Counterfactual History and Economic Growth

But as they stand, it remains difficult for historians to comprehend the implications for the long-term growth of Britain, America and Russia that might be drawn from estimates of social savings presented in these monographs. Their difficulties may be compounded by Fishlow's disagreement with Fogel's results for 1890. Fishlow observed: 'What made railroad carrying services ultimately dispensable was the prior development of two other innovations, the canal and the steamboat. These lowered transport costs far more than the railroad in its turn.' But, he continued,

> Railroad direct benefits were beginning to make a difference by 1860, and that era laid the foundation for later resource saving of quite substantial proportions. The growth of output in the 1850's when railroad transport services began to overshadow those of canals and steamboats foreshadowed even greater future dominance.

Fishlow's argument is directed to demonstrating that Fogel's estimate of 4.7 per cent of gross national product is possibly a consider-

able understatement of direct gains from railroads. Differences between
the two stem partly from their divergent definitions of social savings.
Fogel's counterfactual economy contains some 5,000 miles of new canals,
improved roads and a shift in the margin of cultivation, while Fishlow's
ceteris paribus assumption precludes any allowance for potential adjustments to the closure of railroads. But Fishlow is also sceptical about
the data employed by Fogel to calculate water and waggon rates per
ton mile and is critical of the multiplier of 4 Fogel used to extrapolate
social savings for the carriage of agricultural produce to freight as a
whole (but on that problem see Appendix 1).

Since both authors accept the proposition that benefits from railroads increased over time, it may be difficult to reconcile their estimates.
Either Fishlow's ratio for social savings of 3.3 per cent of national
product in 1859 is too high or Fogel's 4.7 per cent for 1890 is too low.
The following analysis and arithmetic attempts to bring out essential
differences between the *ceteris paribus* counterfactual, favoured by
Fishlow and others, as an approximation to a controlled experiment,
and Fogel's counterfactual, where the economy adjusts to the absence
of the railroad and which is offered as a more plausible and realistic
specification on the American economy without railroads. The discussion should also help students to appreciate the difficulties involved
in drawing inferences about the impact of railways on long-term
development from estimates of social savings.

For expository purposes I propose to manufacture a *guess* of what
the shut-down of railroads not simply in 1859 but over the entire
period of 31 years from 1859 to 1890 might imply for level of output
in 1890. Again I operate on a restricted set of *ceteris paribus* assumptions that are more or less plausible. I assume that America's railroad
system was totally destroyed in 1859 and no attempt was made to
rebuild until after 1890. The immediate effect of destruction would
be a fall of 3.3 per cent in national product — Fishlow's estimate of
the cost in real terms to maintain the volume and pattern of freight
flows without the railroad. I also assume that the trend rate of growth
for the American economy would have remained at the observed rate
of 4 per cent over this period. In other words if the American economy
had lost the use of railroads for 31 years, nothing else would change
and the system would have adjusted and all other factors promoting
growth in America would have maintained the economy on a long-term
growth path where national output increased at 4 per cent per year.
This assumption that growth would have continued at roughly the
same rate with or without the railroad seems to be in line with general

conclusions favoured by new economic historians, namely that competitive systems do find substitutes for innovations often regarded by older economic historians as prerequisites for long-term development.

Year after year between 1859 and 1890 the absence of railways would impose losses on the American economy equivalent to the output foregone as the system diverted resources from the production of consumers' and producers' goods in order to cope with additions to the volume of freight made available for transhipment as a consequence of the growth in total output. These losses depend upon the increase in the volume of freight that would have been carried by railroads, if they had *not* been destroyed in 1859. I conservatively assume that freight carried by rail would have grown at the same rate as national product, namely 4 per cent a year from 1859 to 1890. This assumption contains a downward bias because over time railroads supplied more ton miles to shippers of freight not only because more freight became available to be shipped around America but also because the railroad would presumably become steadily more efficient and competitive compared with second best alternatives such as roads and waterways. Of course, it is also plausible to hypothesise that improvement over time takes place in both rail and non-rail transportation and that without railways the pressure to increase the efficiency of haulage by boat and waggon would have intensified and there is no reason, *a priori*, to expect the gap in relative efficiency to widen. But it seems more reasonable to argue that the technological potential for reductions in real costs was greater for railroads than for other forms of transport and that the share of freight sent by rail would have risen year by year over the period 1859 to 1890.

The following tabulations utilise the calculations of social savings published by Fishlow and Fogel just to illustrate what *might* have happened to the American economy deprived of railroads between 1859 and 1890 and to exemplify the nature of counterfactual speculation, even when backed with sophisticated support from economic theory.

Table 1 Social Savings and American Growth, 1859-90: Some Counterfactual Speculations

	1 4% Growth	2 3.76% Growth	3 3.84% Growth
1859	100.0	96.7	96.7
1890	337.3	303.5	311.0

Column 1 is the actual trend growth rate for the American economy of 4 per cent per annum.

Column 2 is designed to represent hypothetical growth without railroads and with no adjustments — a *ceteris paribus* condition favoured by Fishlow, Hawke and Metzer. If American railroads had been destroyed in 1859 national product would fall in that year by 3.3 per cent (Fishlow's estimate for social savings). Thereafter the extra costs of coping without railroads would rise in the counter-factual economy as the steadily increasing volume of freight was, hypothetically speaking, shifted from railroads onto boats and waggons and as the relative efficiency of roads and waterways declined compared to railroads.

Another way of seeing it would be to perceive that some proportion of the resources deployed to produce the increment to total output that accrued to America with railroads would be required to sustain transport services for a counterfactual America deprived of railroads. Thus every year a bundle of resources with an opportunity cost of 'r' would be employed in transport. That cost would rise from 3.3 per cent above the actual cost of sending freight with railroads in 1859 (Fishlow's estimate) to 8.8 per cent in 1890 (as deduced from Fogel's unadjusted estimate for social savings for that year). On average, over the 31 years from 1859 to 1890 the extra costs of maintaining transport services without railroads would be $\frac{3.3\% + 8.8\%}{2}$ or 6.05 per cent over the actual cost with railroads. Just over 6 per cent of the increment to output each year would be lost because American producers were compelled to tranship extra freight by waggon and boat instead of by train and this extra cost can be represented as an adjustment to the observed rate of growth between 1859 and 1890; where:

$$Gt + 1 = Gt + \frac{4}{100}.Gt - \frac{r}{100}.\frac{4}{100} Gt$$

$$= Gt (1 + 0.04 - (0.0r) (0.04))$$
$$= Gt (1.04 - (0.0605) (0.04))$$
$$= Gt (1.04 - 0.0024)$$
$$= Gt (1.0376).$$

Thus the rate of growth adjusted for the destruction of railroads could be 3.76 per cent per annum from 1859 to 1890.

GNP might grow as follows:

GNP 1859 = 100 - 3.3% = 96.7
GNP 1890 = 96.7 $(1.0376)^{31}$ = 303.5

Column 3 also represents hypothetical growth without railroads but with adjustments to social savings. It is a *mutatis mutandis* counterfactual of a restricted kind favoured by Fogel. In this hypothetical economy Americans react positively to the destruction of railroads by building canals and improving roads so that the incremental costs of coping without railroads rises from 3.3 per cent in 1859 to only 4.7 per cent in 1890. On average the additional costs of maintaining transport services by waterways and roads would be $\frac{4.7\% + 3.3\%}{2}$ or 4 per cent above the costs of shipping the additional freight that became available with the growth of the economy.

Repeating the calculations set out above with 'r' = 4% or 0.04 produces a growth rate of 3.84% and a GNP for 1890 of 311.0.

These counterfactual exercises and their attendant hypothetical numbers are included here to exemplify differences between two versions of the counterfactual employed in the new economic history of railways. Unfortunately there is no logical basis for choice between them. The exercise also illustrates the very real difficulties of trying to deploy estimates of social savings in discussions of the relationship between railways and economic growth in Britain, America or Russia.

For example, if the estimates refer solely to the costs of sustaining transport services at a given level during a shut-down for one year and to nothing else, they cannot be used without ambiguity to rebut the 'exaggerated' and crudely quantified claims made by Rostow and others for the contributions made by railroads to economic development over the long run. If, however, new economic historians wish to go beyond the very limited inferences that can, apparently, be drawn from the quantified cost of closure over a single year, to argue (as Fogel seems inclined to in one of his statements) that social savings is 'a measure of the extent to which railroads increased the production potential of the economy (i.e. shifted the economy's production possibilities function)' counterfactual speculation becomes relevant but far more problematical.

The hypothetical numbers set out above refer only to the central gains that accrued to an economy from railroads as providers of more efficient transport services in the carriage of freight. In this sense and in a long-term counterfactual situation where a country is prevented from exploiting its most efficient form of transport, extra resources would be required year after year to cope with the task of moving freight along roads and waterways, freight which would in the real world have been moved by rail. The precise effects of this hypothetical diversion of resources into the transport sector over time cannot be measured because it all depends (as Fogel recognises) upon how the economy might have adjusted to the absence of a technically superior mode of transport. On a *ceteris paribus* assumption (i.e. an assumption of no adjustments) the rate of growth may have fallen from 4 per cent to 3.76 per cent, a fall sufficient to have reduced national output to 90 per cent of the observed level for 1890.

Perhaps it is more plausible to predict (pace Fogel) that an economy without railroads would have realigned the location of economic activity, altered structure of production and improved transport by road and water in order to minimise the extra costs of coping without railroads. Working with his measure of adjustments postulated for 1890 it is possible to guess that the growth from 1859 to 1890 rate might have fallen from 4 per cent to 3.84 per cent and that the level of GNP for the latter year might have been as much as

8 per cent below the level reached with railways.

Adjustments and substitutions could, in theory, offset all the disadvantages of coping with a second best technique of production and the rate of growth may have remained at the observed level without railways. In a hypothetical economy all sorts of assumptions can be entertained and supported in terms of the existing corpus of economic theory. Historians might even speculate (as Fogel does) about alternative paths of technical progress in transport and predict the earlier development of the internal combustion engine. The arithmetic set out above provides a guess of what might have happened to America's growth rate if the economy had been compelled to manage without railroads from 1859 to 1890, on *ceteris paribus* and other more plausible and less restrictive assumptions. The exercise made no attempt to measure the impact on the growth rate of coping without railroads from 1840 to 1859. Nor was any note taken of externalities, or backward and forward linkages from railroads, that raised the total volume of resources and the national output over time. Those particular effects will be dealt with in Chapters 4 to 6.

On the assumptions specified it still looks as if the failure to take advantage of an innovation as important as railroads might have had a 'real' impact on the growth of the British, American and Russian economies. Furthermore, that impact was almost certainly far larger than the costs of closure for one year in 1890 (i.e. 4.7 per cent of GNP) unless the American economy made a range of adjustments and substitutions for railroads that are difficult to envisage and, by definition, impossible to validate. We may agree with Cootner that 'railroads never made a difference between growth and stagnation' but even the most notional quantification of their importance is still elusive. Estimates of social savings, formulated and quantified with great ingenuity by new economic historians of railways, can only be used to make rather limited points in discussions of the relationship between railways and economic growth.

4 SOCIAL RATES OF RETURN ON INVESTMENT IN RAILWAYS

1 Consumers' Surplus

If they could be calculated social rates of return on investment seem
to provide historians with better numbers for appreciating the *relative*
contribution of railways to economic growth in the nineteenth century.
As David observed:

> Were railroads found to have offered a differentially high rate
> of return . . . one would have to acknowledge that the innova-
> tion made a positive contribution to the economy's growth. The
> importance of that contribution, however, can only be judged
> properly by reference to both the size of the differential social
> rate of return and the volume of real savings that could have
> been absorbed in railroad investment before the differential
> vanished.

Tabulated alongside social rates of return obtained from investment
in other innovations, such estimates for railways would help us to rank
their importance in the growth process and would tell historians if real
national income in America, Britain and Russia could have grown more
or less rapidly with increased or reduced investment in railways.
Fishlow, Nerlove, David and Hawke all calculated social rates of return
and their estimates have been subjected to a rigorous critique by
McClelland and others. Furthermore, the empirical and logical objections to estimates used to measure the gains from investment in railroads (within an exercise designed to measure the social rate of return
on this investment) are valid *pari passu* as objections to estimates of
social savings expressed as a share of national income. Benefits are
conceptually equivalent for both exercises. Students of economics
should not be surprised to discover that many of the major difficulties
in the application of cost benefit to project selection in a modern
economy also emerged when those same concepts were deployed to
evaluate investment in railways in the nineteenth century. Nevertheless, a survey of the debate will bring out some of the problems
involved when new economic historians tried to assess the contribution
of any major innovation to the long term growth of Britain, America

and Russia.

Gains in social welfare from the introduction of railways were divided between three groups: the consumers of transport services (that is to say those producers who shipped commodities by rail, and those who ultimately consumed those same commodities), those who supplied railway services, and all others in society who benefitted indirectly from the diffusion of this important innovation. Cost benefit analysis attempts to conceptualise and measure these gains by relating them to gross investment in a given innovation or project.

$$S = \frac{CS + GR - OE - D + Y}{GI}$$ is a standard version of the accountancy framework used to construct estimates for the average social rate of return on a given investment. (For my heuristic purposes I ignore the complications of transforming a stream of gains that accrued over time into present values.) For a given gross investment in railways (GI) CS is the addition to consumer surplus, that is the additional benefits derived by consumers of transport services; GR - OE - D attempts to define the benefits derived by those who supplied railway services to the economy (producers' surplus) as gross operating receipts (GR) minus operating expenses (OE) minus the depreciation on capital invested in railways (D). Y includes all additional benefits, externalities, positive and negative, which accrued to other social groups and enterprises in the economy from the operation of the railways over one year.

For McClelland and other critics of the new economic history of railways the key defect is a reliance on social savings (as estimated) as a proxy for the benefit to consumers (the addition to consumer surplus) that came about from the fall in the price of transport which resulted from the introduction of the railway.

Consumers' surplus can be defined in text-book manner as the maximum consumers will pay for a service minus the amount actually paid. It might be intuitively grasped as the total sum that producers could extract from consumers of their goods and services before the quantity consumed fell to zero. Diagrammatically it is represented by the area below the demand curve, DBP[1] in the figure below, which will be used to elucidate this serious objection to the published estimates of social savings, namely that they cannot serve as proxies for consumers' surplus. Nor, to extend the argument, can social savings as estimated be identified with the extra income made available to society by the inputs released from the transport sector for production elsewhere in the economy.

The following diagram adapted from Mishan's well known text on cost benefit analysis should make the theoretical basis of this fundamental critique explicit. The diagram represents a historial situation where British, American and Russian producers were initially offered carriage for their goods by waterways and roads only and were subsequently offered a cheaper alternative by rail. Let us call the initial situation a Canal Age and the latter period a Railway Age.

Benefits to Consumers from Investment in Railways

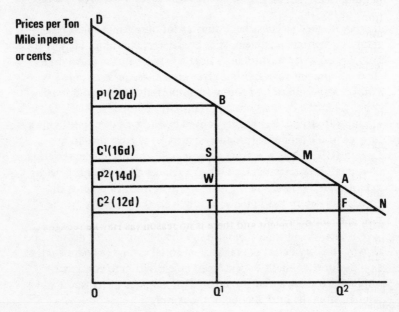

The Canal Age

Canal companies charge producers P^1 or 20d per ton mile. Their average costs of moving freight are, however, 16d per ton mile. Consumer surplus is equal to the triangle $P^1 DB$. Quasi rents are 4d per ton mile, represented by the rectangle $P^1 BSC^1$.

The Railway Age

Railway companies charge P^2 or 14d per ton mile. Their average costs of moving freight come to 12d per ton mile which includes capital costs or the return that railway investment could earn in some alternative set of projects. Canal companies drop their price per ton mile to C^1 in order to compete with railways.

Consumers surplus is now represented by the triangle P^2DA. Quasi rents earned by railway companies are 2d per ton mile, represented by the rectangle C^2P^2AF.

Benefits from the Introduction of Railways

Benefits or gains in welfare should be measured as the reduction in costs from 16d per ton mile by canal to 12d per ton mile by rail, represented by C^1C^2TS, plus the additional freight carried (the shift in ton miles from Q^1 to Q^2) as a result of the fall in freight charges from 20d to 14d, equivalent to the triangle BWA, plus the profits made by railway companies on the additional ton miles of freight carried by rail ($P^2 - C^2$ or 2d per ton mile) represented by the rectangle TWAF.

Estimated Social Savings and Real Gains from Railways

In a perfectly competitive economy with prices equal to average costs, social savings measured as $(C^1 - C^2)Q^2$ would be the correct measure of benefits derived from the introduction of railways — a measure that is represented by the rectangle C^1C^2NM.

The figures employed to calculate social savings by Fishlow, Hawke and others are $(C^1 - P^2)Q^2$ which is clearly not equivalent. Furthermore, C^1 is the price charged by canal companies in order to compete with railways for freight and there is no reason (as Hawke recognised) to expect the quasi rents embodied in the prices initially charged by canals to fall in an economy deprived of railways. McClelland is surely correct to conclude that any measure of consumers surplus based upon $(C^1 - P^2)Q^2$ 'is therefore suspect to the point of being unacceptable'.

2 Opportunity Costs

Since the income gain is equivalent under competitive conditions to the reduction in the real costs of transport, social savings also purport to measure the costs to the economy of the additional resources that would have to be employed in haulage by water and road if the trains had stopped running. The term costs refer to 'opportunity cost', that is, to the value of output sacrificed by employing resources in haulage by waggon and boat rather than, say, in agriculture, or industry. Given plausible estimates for the total miles of road and water transport required to ship the goods actually carried on trains, the difference in costs between the efficient and second best alternative is indeed the cost to an economy from the closure of railways. The estimates pre-

sented by Fishlow and Fogel refer, however, to *charges* made by
railways compared to *charges* made by hauliers by road and water
and their problem was to ascertain the degree to which the rates per
ton mile charged by railroads and the tariffs published for waggon
and boat haulage represented the opportunity cost per ton mile of
moving freight in 1859 and 1890. Neither Fogel nor Fishlow deal in
detail with the probable deviation of tariff rates from marginal cost
for the transport industry — an industry whose pricing policy so often
departs from the norms of competitive equilibrium. Both authors
preferred to adopt the convenient assumption that the transport
system in 1859 and 1890 operated under competitive conditions
and that tariffs published for those years reflected the 'real' costs
of transporting freight. Their reluctance to consider possible correc-
tions to actual prices (which were, in any case, difficult enough to
find) is understandable because adjustments would involve them in
the task of estimating quasi rents (including the prices charged to
send goods by rail, water and road). The possible permutations
and likely direction of bias would be impossible to assess.

Another glance at the graph will illustrate the point. In the
Canal Age canal companies charge producers P^1 or 20d per ton
mile and earn quasi rents of 4d a ton mile, represented by $P^1 BSC^1$.
Come the Railway Age railway companies charge P^2 or 14d a ton
mile. Their real costs are C^2 or 12d a ton mile. Canals compelled
to compete for freight charge C^1 or 16d a ton mile, equivalent to
their real costs of operation. The figures required to calculate the real
savings in resources from the introduction of railways are $C^1 - C^2$
equivalent to 4d per ton mile. Published tariff rates used by Fogel
and Fishlow will give $C^1 - C^2$ equal on the graph to 2d per ton mile.
Two related points are established here: one is that all sorts of
assumptions are possible about quasi rents. More generally it seems
that the use of price data related to years when railways had become
established as serious competitors to roads and waterways will inevitably produce rather low estimates of social savings because
hauliers by boat and waggon will reduce their prices and even cut
their costs in order to compete with railways. Competition between
different forms of carrier should eventually push the rates per ton
mile charged by road, rail or water towards equality. The persistence
of price differentials will reflect the absence or weakness of competition between the available transport media. Alternatively they
will reflect the degree to which railways offered a superior quality
service for the carriage of freight — superior in terms of speed and regu-

larity of movement. These advantages which railways undoubtedly
possessed over their slower, less regular and more risky rivals would
be reflected in tariffs charged by railways — tariffs which could be
raised above the rates charged by hauliers by water, but which
would operate to reduce the estimated value of social savings and
necessitate a separate and rather difficult calculation of the gains
from speed, regularity and reduced risk. Such calculations have,
however, been undertaken by the new economic history of railways,
and the difficulties of that exercise will be reviewed below.

For his calculation of social savings Metzer employed the rates fixed
by the Russian Government for the railways system and the market
prices charged by hauliers who used waggons and boats. He argued that
the official tariff for the shipment of freight by rail did not embody
quasi rents or monopoly profits and in fact fell below the marginal costs
of providing the service to producers. Metzer observed:

> This implies that if there is any bias in the cost of rail transport
> that stems from using rates instead of marginal costs, it would
> be an upward bias, which would tend to reinforce the upper-
> limit nature of the social saving estimate. If the official rates are
> below marginal costs the real costs of transhipping freight by
> rail must be understated and that must generate an estimate of
> social savings below the saving in real resources by railways.

Metzer goes on to argue that Russian water and waggon services were
competitive industries with no barriers to entry, and thus the rates
charged by these industries approximate to the real costs of the
resources they used. But White writing on the same subject thought
that 'in a situation of disguised unemployment the opportunity cost
of labour employed in providing carting services is zero or rather
the loss of leisure time'. Thus in White's view the rates charged to carry
freight by road and water probably overstated the opportunity cost
of the labour and other inputs employed in traditional transport. If
White is correct this bias will also operate to produce an estimate of
social savings that overstates the real benefits of railways. Thus it
seems that, *ceteris paribus,* the biases in the price data used by Metzer
serve to exaggerate the savings in real resource that emanated from the
introduction of railways in Russia.

Hawke is exempt from these objections because he presents figures
of the real costs per ton mile of shipping freight along just two water-

ways — the Leeds and Liverpool and the Kennet and Avon canals.
This does not, however, really circumvent the problem of what
canals and waggons *would* have charged producers in an economy
deprived of the services of railways. Historians may be prepared to
accept that published tariffs for carriage by road, water and rail
could serve as a rough approximation to marginal costs, but serious
difficulties of finding 'facts' for the counterfactual economy would
persist. For example, they will enquire what could happen to costs
per ton mile as millions of tons of freight are shifted from railways
to roads and waterways?

Fishlow argued that America possessed the capacity to cope with
large-scale shifts of freight off the railroads. He is, however, impelled
to admit:

> As the demand for transportation by horse and waggon, say,
> approaches some critical total, the cost of bidding resources
> away from other sectors might well prove to increase rapidly.
> Or with expanded canal utilisation, there might be a sharp dis-
> continuity due to lack of sufficient capacity.

Both Fishlow and Fogel argued that the excess capacity available
on waterways in 1859 and 1890 made it likely that freight diverted
from railroads could be sent by boat at a constant real cost per ton
mile. As far as costs for the use of waterways as such are concerned,
the assumption may be defensible — but for roads it seems less
plausible; and as for the costs involved in the hire of shipping space,
horses and waggons, as well as the costs of attracting additional
labour into haulage, the assumption may turn out to be unrealistic.

Metzer also recognised that the published rates per ton mile

> might not accurately reflect the cost involved in shipping the
> railroads freight by water and overland in 1907. Such a dis-
> crepancy might, in principle, be the outcome of a rising marginal
> cost function in water (and waggon) transportation and/or the
> possibility that the actual rates on the 'surviving' (and obviously
> most efficient) waterways were actually lower than the water
> rates that would have existed in the absence of railroads.

He cites a statistical yearbook to support his contention 'that the
available water rate statistics clearly imply constant marginal costs . . .'
Over what range of time and rate of increases in tonnage is not

specified. But he does argue that:

> Unlike the United States, where freight shipments on waterways
> would have increased by 400 per cent in the absence of railways
> in 1890, in Russia freight ton-mileage on water would have risen by
> 150 per cent only. This relatively small increase of shipments justi-
> fies the extension of the constant marginal cost assumption to the
> additional ton-mileage that would have been accommodated in the
> absence of railways in 1907.

The increase in shipments may have been small relative to the increment for the United States, but was it small compared to the capacity
of waterways to operate at constant costs over one year while the railways were shut down? But if White is correct and the resources used in
cartage had very low opportunity cost the assumption of constant marginal cost in that sub-sector of transport may well be correct for labour
but improbable with respect to animals employed, such as horses and
oxen.

Hawke is the only new economic historian who seriously defends
the assumption of constant costs with the aid of published figures. He
cited figures, again from the Leeds-Liverpool and the Kennet-Avon
canals, in order to show that costs per ton mile did not rise as the
volume of freight carried along those particular canals increased.

Unfortunately, a scrutiny of Hawke's graphs reveals that he cannot
derive unambiguous support for his assumption. For some years costs
increased less rapidly than tons transported along the canals, but for
other years costs increased more rapidly. In any case the evidence is
just not sufficient to conclude that 'canals would have had approximately constant costs in the range of output relevant to the hypothetical situation'.

The diversion of output from the railways in 1865 would have increased the demand for canal capacity at a rate far beyond that
implied by the increased demand that these two canals coped with over
a far longer time period. The *ceteris paribus* assumption that is so
useful in micro economic theory applies to small changes in output,
but for the kind of massive shifts implied by these exercises in counterfactual history that kind of assumption seems untenable. Hawke is too
good an economist not to be aware of this point and admits the most
likely deviation from the assumption of constant costs is in an upward
direction. But by how much? Nobody can really say or begin to
estimate.

Furthermore, McClelland also shows that other proxies for consumer surplus such as the rise in land rents that occurred as a result of railroad construction — proxies used by Fogel and Mercer in their studies of the Central and Union Pacific Railroads — while theoretically valid are again extremely difficult to measure. Interestingly enough, McClelland's critique duplicates some of the arguments used by Fogel in his rejection of Fishlow's assumption that 'the change of the value of agricultural land between 1850-60 reflects the increase in national income attributable to railroads.' As Fogel saw it the conditions examined by Fishlow required the employment of a general equilibrium model, and:

> Under such conditions the change in agricultural rent arising
> from a reduction in transport costs may be less than, greater than
> or equal to the change in income originating in agriculture. Indeed
> it is entirely possible that the effects of railroads per se was to reduce
> land rents and that the observed rise is attributable entirely to the
> increase in capital and labour that took place.

In McClelland's words:

> To deduce the effect of railroad construction only, one must
> correct observed changes in land values for the effects of movements
> in the general price level shifts in the aggregate demand for agricul-
> tural products, increases in real farm investment and other relevant
> changes in supply conditions.

In empirical terms this task does seem beyond the bounds of possibility.

3 Indirect costs

Railways also provided producers with a range of indirect benefits which can be defined and quantified as the saving in real resources that accrued from their greater speed, regularity, safety and immunity from climatic obstruction compared to carriers by road and water. The specification and measurement of these benefits are amoung the most impressive contributions of the new economic history of transport.

Fogel and Fishlow very astutely suggested that proxies for the saving in real resources could be obtained by identifying the steps that producers might take to mitigate the effects of a railway shut down. For example, to safeguard their interests against the additional losses (that inevitably occurred in the shipment of freight by boat and waggon) producers would pay extra insurance premiums, and the increment to their insurance bills could be used as an outer-bound estimate of the gains that came to an economy from the greater reliability of railroads.

Boats and waggons were both slower than trains. In America, and still more in Russia, they could be idle for long periods of the year when extremes of cold or heat made roads and waterways impassable.. Russian waterways, for example, were frozen for six months of the year. Inclement conditions did not, however, affect British transport to anything like that extent. Again, Fogel and Fishlow saw that enterprises could safeguard production and distribution against the slower and discontinuous flow of intermeditate and final output from their suppliers, simply by holding higher levels of stocks: thus the extra storage costs and interest charges incurred as producers raised the ratio of stocks to output in the counterfactual economy provided evidence for the estimation of the costs of resources required to substitute for the advantages obtained from the fast and more continuous service supplied by railways. These charges (the costs of time and insurance) form a high proportion of the costs of coping without railroads.

Critics argued that Fogel understated the capital required for storage capacity needed to hold stocks of industrial raw materials, grain and livestock (particularly the last). The shorter season of transport by road and water also implied that more boats and waggons would be required in season in order to hurry freight to its final destination. In winter this capacity would be idle and would increase costs per ton mile for an economy deprived of railways. This cost seems to have been ignored in the assumption that commodities could be reallocated onto boats and waggons at a constant marginal cost.

An accurate assessment of the additional interest and storage charges incurred in the counterfactual economy can only be constructed commodity by commodity. For some commodities, like grain, where output is seasonal, the absence of trains would involve only a shift in stocks between suppliers and distributors with perhaps no change in the ratio of stocks to output and only a small addition to the social costs of holding inventories. For fresh meat, fish, dairy and other perishable farm produce, it is, however, difficult to envisage substitutes for the rapid and continuous flow between farmers and producers provided by railways. Perhaps the effect of railways upon investment in stocks and storage capacity is most obvious for minerals and manufactured goods where the innovation certainly promoted the transformation of circulating into fixed capital. Nevertheless, the exercises in

quantification in these monographs do provide estimates of the
impact of railways upon the ratio of stocks to national income
that go well beyond simple identification and intuitive measurement.

4 Externalities

Even to measure the gains to consumers as well as to the suppliers
of services provided by railways for one year poses formidable data
problems. Proxies for real costs in the form of current prices seem to
leave the way open to interpretations that may well make the estimates
of social savings ambiguous indicators of the additional resources required to cope with a shut-down over one year and dubious measures
of the real gains required in cost benefit analysis. But even if more
acceptable estimates of these 'private' benefits could be formulated,
the omission of externalities from Fishlow and Hawke's calculations
of the average social rate of return on capital invested in American
and British railways as well, as the absence of an appropriate standard
for comparison with such a rate of return, makes it difficult to assess
the contribution of railways.

Problems related to the identification and measurement of externalities and the conflation of private returns and social benefits are
commonplace in recent controversies over the applicability of cost
benefit analysis to resource allocation in underdeveloped countries.
New economic historians also found it impossible to quantify externalities. But David, Fishlow and Hawke made no attempt to conceal
either the omission of externalities from their estimates of social
savings, or any assumptions they made which equated private and
social benefits. Hawke admits candidly that 'the study of linkages
from railways indicates that the quantitive measurement of social
returns to investment in railways results in an underestimate.' Most
of Fishlow's book is concerned to analyse the mechanisms through
which social returns from railways exceeded its private profitability
and recognised that 'because of their wide variety of consequences'
his calculation of 'returns to capital in the shape of net earnings and
transport cost savings alone' was 'inevitably partial'. He was, moreover, inclined to come down on the side of larger indirect effects
and 'this suggests a social rate of return to railroad investment well
above 20 per cent and indeed, close to 30 per cent' – that is double
his original estimate of 15 per cent.

White seems disposed to rank gains in the form of externalities that flowed from investment in Russian railroads above the direct benefits that accrued from the provision of cheaper transport. But Metzer argued that the Russian economy may have been too backward to take advantage of the potentialities of railways and that externalities may have been more important in the United States. He generalised: 'the application of technological innovations in the infrastructure might have a greater direct economic impact in an advanced economy than a less developed one, which might not be able to realise their full benefits.'

New economic historians have certainly come up with original information and hypotheses about externalities. They definitely differ in the importance they ascribe qualitatively to such benefits. Fishlow and White are inclined to rank such gains as equal to or above direct benefits. Fogel, Hawke and Metzer tend to argue that most of the benefits from railroads are captured in their estimates of social savings and are not disposed to impute much importance to externalities. Disputes about externalities are usually about the relative importance of benefits from investment that neo-classical economics finds extremely difficult to measure. This observation is not, however, an argument against pushing quantification as far as possible and as the standard *Manual* by Little and Mirlees suggests 'mentioning such possibilities in a qualitative or literary manner'. Fishlow and Hawke seem to have followed that advice and economic historians cannot be expected to do better than their colleagues in economics working on contemporary problems of resource allocation. The whole subject will, in any case, be dealt with as forward and backward linkages in Chapters 5 and 6.

5 Social and Other Rates of Return

As we noticed earlier an appropriate standard for comparison is a problem both for estimates of social rates of return and for social savings. The advantage of social rates of return is that such a measure does at least systematically relate the benefits from the diffusion of an innovation to the investment required to bring it to fruition. Fishlow put the rate of return on capital invested in American railroads before the Civil War at about 15 per cent a year and argued that 'only an alternative investment with a larger return over this span would have led to higher incomes than actually observed with railroads'. It is difficult, he maintained, 'to imagine the country doing much better than that in any reasonable alternative. The immediate stream of private benefits means that only if the harvest of indirect, social gains, were higher elsewhere could the ante-bellum company have done as well as in their absence'. Hawke compared his estimate for the social internal rate of return (15 per cent − 20 per cent for 1830-70) with the yield on console and the discount rate on first class three month bills and held: 'Although it would be desirable to have estimates of the rate of return in other industries between 1830 and 1870, there can be little doubt that railways provided socially advantageous investment opportunities'. While Mercer's reference for comparison is the 'annual average earnings − price ratio of all stock on the New York Stock Exchange for 1871-1889'.

McClelland is sceptical about all available standards for comparison either because they compare private with social returns or (more significantly) because:

> a social rate of return on investment alternatives against which the performance of the railroad can be gauged has yet to be made for the 19th century. Measures of social rates . . . of the order of 15 per cent to 20 per cent cannot, therefore, be taken as prima facie evidence of superior economic benefits being created for the community by this form of investment.

Fishlow's 'guess' for a rate of return which included externalities comes to 20 per cent to 30 per cent. Investment in transport is thought to generate considerable external benefits, and it may be relevant to include a reference to Weiss and Bateman's estimated rate of return of about 30 per cent on investment in Southern manufacturing industry for 1860.

McClelland's position on this particular issue simply reflects agnosticism in the face of assumptions found to be necessary if cost benefit analysis is to be undertaken anywhere at any time. Theoretical purity should not be retained at all costs and it is surely essential for economists and economic historians to adjust observed market prices in order to bring them closer to social opportunity costs. And it is also permissible to devise proxies in order to calculate the social rate of return on investment. 'True' accounting prices and social rates of return on capital will never be available for the nineteenth century but that is no reason to check the search for answers to important questions about social gains from the allocation of resources, provided more acceptable estimates for consumers and producers surplus could be calculated.

If that could be accomplished, measured returns on investment in railways would represent lower bound estimates for the social rates of return. Potential gains from externalities and linkages of all kinds could then be analysed and listed alongside measured benefits. Reference could be made to rates of return on feasible alternative forms of capital formation — again with quantification pushed to its limits and unmeasured benefits placed into the equation for comparison. Modern planners proceed in this way and historians must expect to do no better. Finally, since new economic history is concerned to measure the relative importance of selected innovations in long-term development, a ranking of innovations in terms of their average social rates of return appears to be indispensable and it seems to constitute a theoretically more viable indicator than social savings expressed as a proportion of gross national product.

This argument is not, moreover, vulnerable to McClelland's further objection that *average* rates of return would not provide satisfactory answers to the question of whether a given community invested too much or too little in railways. For that particular question marginal rates of return are required, but for a broad appraisal of the *relative* importance of railways an average rate will probably suffice, unless the historian happens to be interested in the rationality of adding to the capital stock embodied in railways at particular moments of time. To build up a railway system the community took a whole series of investment decisions, and calculations, like those of Fishlow and Hawke of average rate of return for railways as a whole over a span of time, include a dispersion of returns upon quite discrete extensions to the rail network and its capital stock.

Marginal rates of return on investment in railroads are, however, certainly required to support David's conclusion that 'from a social viewpoint, by 1890 further investment in railroad transportation capacity did not constitute an especially advantageous way of using US resources'. David's method of calculating the net and gross marginal social rates of return on investment in American railroads for 1890 made use of all the familiar assumptions for the derivation of marginal productivities in production function analysis. In his words:

> assuming there is an aggregate production function for the railroad industry, and, further, that strict proportionality exists between the social and private output of that industry, the marginal social productivity of capital may be estimated as the product of the

average social productivity of capital and the elasticity of private
output with respect to capital.

The derivation of this elasticity involved further assumptions, namely,
a production function for railroads that exhibited constant returns to
scale and where private returns to capital was equal to its private
marginal value product. Under such conditions the elasticity of private
output with respect to capital in 1890 is given by the share of capital
at that date.

Such assumptions may well be treated with the kind of scepticism
that neo-classical production theory now meets from the pens of
Cambridge economists. But until Cambridge controversies over the
theory of capital are more settled, economic historians may or may
not feel free to adopt such assumptions when measuring the marginal
productivity of capital and thus may or may not accept David's
conclusion that, 'by 1890 the margin of railroad capital formation in
the US had already been pushed close to the point of exhausting any
differential social returns afforded by exploitation of the
innovation.'

In any case, the marginal rate of return on capital invested in railways over a single year tells us very little about the overall importance
of railways compared to other innovations that were exploited for
the long-term benefit of the American, British and other economies.

5 FEEDBACKS FROM RAILWAYS

1 The Nature of Feedbacks

From the time of their establishment, the expenditures of railway companies upon labour, raw materials, capital goods and industrial inputs also exercised cumulative effects upon the growth of national economies. The new economic history of railways observed that since the estimate of social savings are based upon the actual transport flows for 1859, 1865, 1890 and 1907 and those flows reflect the growth of national output, social savings (externalities apart) includes most of the gains to the economies of America, Russia and Britain that emanated from expenditures by railway companies. But in order to isolate feedbacks from railways to growth a rigorous exercise in counterfactual history would presumably contrast and quantify the effects of such expenditures upon long-term development with the impact of hypothetical outlays by substitute carriers employed by producers deprived of the services of railways. While the logic of this injunction is recognised, empirically the research could not be pursued. Instead new economic historians concentrated upon analysing the impact of railway expenditures upon trends and fluctuations in national income. They then went on to measure the effects on particular industries that flowed from demand by railways for their products.

2 Railway Investment and Fluctuations in National Income

Fogel's study, concerned with 'unique attributes' of railroads, contains no discussion of connections between capital formation in railroads and changes in aggregate demand, but Fishlow, Hawke and Fenoaltea (writing about Italian railways) devote full attention to this particular macro relationship. Hawke and Fishlow tabulated the share of investment in railways (net and replacement expenditure) to gross domestic capital formation and show that for peak years, like 1847 in England, and 1854 in America, the ratio rose to about 25 per cent. Such careful tabulations enable us to locate groups of years or cycles when investment in railways assumed importance for the overall level of economic activity.

For example, Reed's careful analysis of the pattern of railway

development leads him to observe 'railway companies were a major
element in the speculative booms, and the railway construction
initiated by the legislation of 1836 and 1837 played an important
role in creating home demand and sustaining the economy during
the years of recession'.

Hawke accepts Mathews' tentative conclusion that 'railways are
the main element of the . . . booms of 1835-36 and 1838-40 and in
the severity of the depression of 1841-42'. However, his own analysis
disputes the accepted view that 'in the commercial crisis of 1847
railways were a stabilising factor'. His figures also indicate that 'in
the boom of the 1860's an increased share of fixed capital formation
was performed by railways, but in the boom of the 1870's while
railway investment increased, the rise in the share of investment
performed by railways was much less marked'.

Fishlow also traces interconnections between 'volatile' changes
in railway investment and fluctuations in national income. His
analysis brings out clearly the fundamental differences in the
contribution of railroad investment to the downswings of the
1830s and 1850s: 'In the earlier period railroad investment was a
victim not a fundamental cause of the slackening pace of development, whereas in the 1850's the connection ran the other way'.
For Italian industrial growth, Fenoaltea's article concludes: 'time
paths were dominated by the cycle in railway investment largely
synochronous with, and more severe than, the cycle in industrial
output'.

Fenoaltea's more completely specified model of the impact of
railway investment helped him to estimate 'representative percentage
decreases' in national income that would (hypothetically) have
followed from the removal of that investment. The estimates are
entirely sensitive to the assumptions made about propensities to
save and invest but his general hypothesis is that, railways (at least
in Italy) exercised their greatest 'impact through the spending they
set in motion — an impact they would have retained even if the goods
and services so acquired had never been embodied in the infracture'
Fenoaltea's hypothesis is plausible and raises the general question of
what investment expenditures by railways implied for the realised
rates of economic growth in Britain, America, Russia and Italy.

There are two separable elements to this issue. The first is relevant
to growth and the second is a question of whether the timing and
sequence of capital formation in railroads contributed to cyclical
instability. Answers to the latter question could be found at many

levels of aggregation from national income right down to particular
firms. These monographs tackled the problem at a macro level where
Fenoaltea found that his figures 'indicate a mild boost to industry's
cyclical instability'. On the other hand Fishlow and Hawke's qualified
conclusion is that the timing of investment in railways exerted a
contra-cyclical influence upon the level of economic activity in Britain
and America. It helped both to induce booms and to alleviate subsequent depressions. Hawke, for example, observed that 'the main link
between railways construction and fluctuations in economic activity
is, then, that the former generally lagged behind the latter'. In ante
bellum America, however, Fishlow noticed that 'the pace of railroad
expansion was not subject to the frequent reversals shown by total
activity, whether the test be actual levels of investment or their rate
of change'.

But even if their conclusions are accepted the implications of
contra-cyclical expenditure by railways are (as Hawke acutely argued)
not yet clear. Trade cycle theory is rich in hypotheses but until
connections between cycles of capital formation in railways and
economic activity are investigated at the level of industries and even
firms, the relationship between investment cycles and long-term
growth will remain obscure. Meanwhile, these penetrating forays into
the problem supports a tentative conclusion that, over the course of
the cycle, investment expenditure by railways moved in a sequence
that probably induced further economic development.

Moving now from cycles to growth and more specifically to
possible connections between opportunities to invest in railways and
the total volume of investible resources available to an economy,
we can do no better than to quote Fishlow's clear exposition of
the issue:

> At one extreme, if we assume the ready availability of other
> capital absorbing projects, their influence is nil, since total
> expenditures are then independent of railroad investment. On
> the other hand, if we regard railroad investment as a unique
> addition to demand, its absence would wipe out a good part
> of the expansion of the decade.

Fenoaltea's article argues that the Italian economy would not
have adjusted quickly enough to a cut off in railway investment to
avoid a long depression. Fogel's position on the inflow of labour to
America suggests he would be more inclined to Fishlow's first

assumption. Fishlow himself is convinced that railroads definitely attracted both immigrants and foreign capital into the United States. For Russia and Italy the same expectation for capital inflow seems even more credible. Perhaps a closer study of institutions and investors involved in the international capital market will confound sceptics who maintain that capital migrates in search of profit not railways. Historians who study these institutions will not under-estimate the pull of profits but they usually entertain the notion that European investors, banks and other financial houses, weaned on the paper assets of British or French railways, would, up to a point, persist in seeking similar outlets for their funds overseas. Reed, for example, observed: 'railways provided the institutional framework which was adapted, if slowly, for other types of domestic investment, while ... the success of railways at home stimulated British investors to look for similar opportunities overseas'. Only those who believe that nineteenth-century markets for foreign capital functioned along the lines specified in neo-classical models will fail to agree with Fishlow's contention that 'railroad securities were a financial investment that particularly appealed to foreign lenders' — or with White's observation that Russian railways were not only an attractive area for foreign investors but 'could familiarise foreign investors with opportunities for other investment in such a country'. Nevertheless, in the end the question of *just how much* foreign capital would have migrated to Russia, Italy or the United States without railways is simply not answerable. The hypothesis of capital inflows is hardly relevant to Britain but some English historians (if I may quip) might agree that the attraction of unskilled Irish labour into England to work on the construction of railways perhaps added little to the long-term growth of national product.

Similar questions and debates apply to domestic savings where Hawke posed the possibility that 'within the financial sphere of economic activity there is the possibility that railways had an educational role on investors themselves', and that this led to an increased propensity to save, particularly in 1847 and the 1860s. Reed certainly concluded from his study that railway investment from 1820 to 1844 drew 'on new classes of investors from the provinces and profoundly influenced the structure of the capital market'. Fishlow expected that the high ratio of capital to output which characterised investment in railroads, together with the inability of railroad companies to retain a high proportion of their profits for expansion, had the effect of augmenting the share of investment in the national income of the United States before the Civil War; while Chandler and Salisbury show in their article that railroads exercised a very definite influence on institutional developments in the American capital market. For Britain, Hawke is less disposed to accord the demands of railway companies for investible funds much of a role, either in promoting greater efficiency in the capital market or in hastening the introduction of limited liability. Debates on externalities of this kind are likely to remain inconclusive.

3 Railways and Industrialisation

Rostow's contention that railroads acted as a leading sector in America's 'take off' from 1843 to 1860 has been refuted by the new economic history. Fogel estimated that in 1859 just under 4 per cent of net value added in manufacturing industry could be attributed to demand from railroads, and he went on to show that 'the market provided by the non-railroad demand for manufactured commodities would still have resulted in a 230 per cent rise in the output of manufacturing over the years from 1840-59 — as opposed to an increase of 240 per cent with the railroad market'. Fishlow also concluded that 'derived demands a favoured Rostow linkage, although they had positive effects by the 1850's as railroad investment increased, were an insignificant influence earlier' and that 'the causes underlying this industrial breakthrough seem to be independent of the railroad'. For Italy it also appears that deliveries of capital and intermediate goods from industry to railways constituted too small a proportion of final output for 'leading sector' status to be ascribed to railways.

Table 2 Shares of Output Delivered for the Construction and Operation of Railways 1840-1913

Industry	USA (Fogel)	USA (Fishlow)	England & Wales (Hawke)
Pig Iron	6%-15% (1840-60)	5%-21% (1840-60)	5%-13% (1835-69)
Bessemer Steel	50%-87% (1871-90)	80% (1867-80)	
Coal	6% (1840-60) 25% (1921)	2% (1859) 20% (1880, 1890)	2%-14% (1865)
Bricks			30% (1840's)

Industry	USA (Fogel)	USA (Fishlow)	England & Wales (Hawke)
Lumber	1% (1840-60)	3%-10% (1840-60)	-
Transport Equipment	25% (1859 only)	11% (1869 loco-motives only)	-

These figures will certainly help historians to appreciate backward linkages from railroads to industry, but without fully articulated input-output and commodity flow tables the full impact of railway demand cannot be measured: as they stand the ratios capture direct flows, but much less of the indirect deliveries from industry to industry that emanated from railway demand. Furthermore, the data may *(prima facie)* lead to a conclusion that feedbacks from railways to industrialisation can be dismissed as unimportant. But a reading of the dispute between Fishlow and Fogel about the significance that could be attached to railroad demand for domestic pig iron output in the United States between 1840 and 1860 will warn students that such inference would be unwarranted. Resolution of this argument must also await the construction of an input-output table for the American economy in the 1850s, because only then can it be ascertained whether the share of intermediate goods sold by any particular industry to railroads ranked above or below the share sold to any other single sector of the economy. In other words, resolution of the issue of importance requires a ranking of railway and other sources of demand. For development theory the issue is not trivial because studies of inter-industry relations predict that the integration of a manufacturing sector through the flows of commod-ities from industry to industry promotes structural change and shifts to higher levels of productivity. Seen in this context, railways perhaps played no small part in the integration of American or European industry during the nineteenth century.

4 Railways and the Iron and Steel Industry

Meanwhile these statistics and the detailed investigations conducted by Fishlow, Hawke and Fenoaltea testify to the relative importance of linkages between railways and the development of primary metal-lurgy. Several methods of quantifying the relationship between the two industries exist, all of them relevant to particular questions. For example, Hawke and Fogel measured the impact of demand for *rails alone*, which may be germane to questions about rails as such, but the general problem of feedbacks is usually related to the effects of total demand from railways upon two broad sectors of the domestic industry: the blast furnace section involved in producing pig iron, and the rolling mills which transformed an input of crude iron (which is pig iron plus scrap iron) into rails and other rolled iron.

Since railways supplied increasing quantities of scrap metal to the rolling mill and other secondary sectors of the iron industry, their *net* demand for the product of the blast furnace section would be exaggerated by reference to figures of gross tons of iron consumed. Thus in order to measure the demand of railroads for pig iron new economic historians required an estimate for the weight of scrap they generated over time. Hawke and Fogel assumed that depreciated rails were recycled as inputs into the iron industry along a time path of replacement that approximated to a log normal curve. Other hypotheses (for example, Mitchell's that rails had to be replaced after ten years service) are also plausible. The point here is that the assumptions employed about depreciation definitely affect estimates of the timing and magnitude of railway demand for pig iron and have produced somewhat but not radically different measures for the impact of that demand upon the blast furnace industries of Britain and America.

Table 3 Impact of Railroad Demand upon the Blast Furnace Sector of the US Iron Industry, 1840-60

Years	Total Domestic Output of pig iron (000 tons)		Railway Demand in pig iron equivalents (000 tons)	
	Fogel	Fishlow	Fogel	Fishlow
1840-45	2,157	2,059	139	96
1846-50	3,647	3,580	194	308
1851-55	3,399	3,039	468	565
1856-60	4,147	3,700	627	762

Fogel's estimates indicate that from 1856 to 1860 blast furnaces delivered 15 per cent of their output to meet demands that emanated from railroads while Fishlow's figures suggest a ratio of 21 per cent. Most of the discrepancy arises from differences between Fogel's theoretically based hypothesis about the rate of rail depreciation compared to Fishlow's estimates which were 'rooted directly in the financial expenditures for iron reported by individual roads'.

Table 4 Impact of Railway Demand upon the Blast Furnace Sector
of the UK Iron Industry, 1835-69

Years	Total Domestic Output of pig iron (000 tons)	Net Railway Demand for Pig Iron (000 tons)	
		Hawke	Mitchell
1835-43	11,010	666	795
1844-51	15,455	1,942	2,773
1852-59	26,253	1,254	2,261
1860-69	45,286	2,242	3,611

According to Hawke the strongest effects occurred over the cycle
1844-51 when the railways of England and Wales absorbed 13 per cent
of the United Kingdom output of pig iron. Mitchell suggested a ratio
of 18 per cent. Again the discrepancy is interesting to economic
historians and is partly explained by different assumptions about rates
of rail depreciation and also by the fact that Hawke (as he makes
perfectly clear) omits from consideration deliveries of iron for the
construction and maintenance of railways in Scotland and Ireland,
even though his denominator for comparison is total output for the
United Kingdom. Compared to America, the British ratios seem low
because they refer to demand for pig iron for permanent way only
which (on Fishlow's evidence for the United States) could cut the
level of demand for pig iron by around 20 per cent Finally, if the
historian is concerned with the effects of railway demand upon the
growth of the iron industry, the case for excluding *imported* iron
delivered to railways in America and Italy is obvious enough. But for
the British iron and steel industry there seems to be a case for analysing
the impact of demand from domestic and overseas railways together.
In a world market context the relative importance of the effects of
railways would be more pronounced.

Unfortunately, it is difficult to measure the impact of railway
demand upon other parts of the iron industry because output data for
higher stages of iron processing are not available. Fogel's ingenious
solution was to measure output data for iron mills (producing rolled,
slit, sheet and other iron) in terms of the physical input employed in
such processes — namely crude iron, which consists of pig iron plus
scrap iron. I have presented his data together with my adjusted estimates
from figures published by Fishlow and Hawke in a single table in order
to provide students with a rough indication of the effects of railway
demand upon the secondary stages of iron processing.

Table 5 The Share of Crude Iron output absorbed by Railways,
1840-60

| Years | United States | | UK |
	Fogel	Fishlow	Hawke
1840-45	7%	6%	8%
1846-50	10%	9%	16%
1851-55	17%	28%	7%
1856-60	25%	34%	6%

Notes: I have applied Fogel's methods to Fishlow's data and to Hawke's data.
I inflated deliveries of crude iron in Hawke by 20 per cent to allow for
locomotives and freight cars. His figures refer to England and Wales and
I made no allowance for deliveries of crude iron for railways in Scotland
and Ireland.

In the formulation and construction of estimates required to
measure railroad demand for ferrous metal, new economic historians
have successfully presented ratios (net of imports and the effects of
rail replacement) that correct exaggerated claims for the influence of
railways upon primary metals. Their estimates are more useful for
testing that influence upon the blast furnace section of the industry
than upon higher stages of iron transformation. It is, however, a pity
that Fogel's preoccupation with Rostow's leading sector hypothesis
precluded the construction of estimates for decades after the Civil
War when (as Fishlow suspected and as Cootner's evidence shows)
the share of pig and crude iron absorbed by railroads far exceeded pre-
war ratios.

Furthermore there are other ways of presenting backward linkages
and averages of the kind set out above may possibly obscure the role
of railways. It is a cliché to insist that growth takes place at the margin
and an investigation into the significance of railways should be focussed upon shifts in the demand curve for iron and other industrial
products. Then if we simply begin in the 1830s with the fact of an
established and growing iron industry, it could be illuminating to
isolate total sales to railways as part of the *growth* in demand for
ferrous metals.

In this context Rostow and other older economic historians
certainly raised basic questions: what share of the increment to total
output did ferrous metals deliver to railways between 1830 and 1900?
Did such additional demand lead to economies of scale in the industry?
Finally, since industrial growth is cyclical and cumulative, how precisely
did the resources, capacity and incomes created by one cycle of railway

investment influence the development of the iron industry over subsequent cycles?

To begin with the last question, it seems that a better perspective might be obtained if connections between railways and ferrous metals are looked at over time.

Table 6 Domestic Output of Pig Iron with and without Railways, 1840-60 (000 tons)

Years	Total Domestic Output			Domestic Output without Railways		
	USA Fishlow	USA Fogel	U K Hawke	USA Fishlow	Fogel	UK Hawke
1841-5	2,059	2,157	7,325	1,963	2,018	6,754
1846-50	3,580	3,647	8,920	3,272	3,453	7,029
1851-55	3,039	3,399	13,631	2,474	2,834	12,777
1856-60	3,700	4,147	18,241	2,938	3,520	17,244

Notes: I inflated Hawke's totals by 20 per cent to include locomotives and freight cars. Hawke's figures for deliveries exclude Scotland and Ireland.

More sophisticated smoothing techniques could be employed but as it stands the data offered in the new economic history of railways supports several interesting conclusions. First, the expansion of pig iron output during the 1840s in America and the United Kingdom owed little to demand from railways. Secondly, deliveries to railroads definitely mitigated the American downswing in production in the late 1840s and early 1850s. Finally, in Britain, deliveries from blast furnaces for domestic railways constituted a small and declining share of the expansion in output.

Table 7 Domestic Output of Crude Iron with and without Railways, 1840-60 (000 tons)

Years	Total Domestic Output			Domestic Output without Railways		
	USA Fogel	Fishlow	UK Hawke	Fogel	USA Fishlow	UK Hawke
1840-44	1,950	2,080	7,354	1,805	1,965	6,773
1845-49	3,875	3,621	9,075	3,495	3,299	7,610
1850-54	3,395	3,317	13,949	2,810	2,389	12,937
1855-59	4,695	4,189	18,683	3,505	2,773	17,479

Notes: I used Fogel's definition and methods to calculate crude iron output (pig, plus total scrap) and deliveries of crude iron to railways. I inflated Hawke's totals by 20 per cent to include locomotives and freight cars. His figures exclude deliveries for railways in Scotland and Ireland. Fishlow's estimates were adjusted to make his data comparable with Fogel.

These estimates for crude iron production with and without railways bring out the greater impact that railway demand exercised on the transformation of iron beyond the blast furnace stage. For America, the expansion of the 1840s seems almost independent of railroad demand, but in Britain deliveries destined for railways accounted for 48 per cent of the extra output produced from 1840-44 to 1845-49. In America, production of processed iron seems to have been strongly supported by railroad demand in the downswing and there is no mistaking its influence on the expansion of the late 1850s, where perhaps something like half of all additional output took the form of rails, locomotives, freight cars and other equipment for the railroads. Finally, differences between the measures based upon pig and crude iron show that only value-added figures can adequately represent the impact of railway demand upon the iron industry as a whole.

There can be no doubt about the impact of railways upon the Italian steel industry. From the Risorgimento to the First World War extensions and replacements to the national rail network rarely absorbed less than a third of Italy's total steel production. In the United States the 'rail share of steel production fluctuated between 50 per cent and 87 per cent over the years 1871-90, at a time when the share of basic steel products in the output of the iron and steel industry grew rapidly', and, as Cootner's figures indicate, from 1875 to 1890 about a quarter of American pig iron production took the form of steel rails.

Such statistics are, however, but a preface to further questions. For example, how far did changes in demand from railways promote technical progress and push iron and steel industries onto new production functions years before any alternative source of demand might conceivably have emerged in a 'counterfactual' path of national development without railways? Progress in metallurgical technology had, it seems, little to do with railways. Most of the major breakthroughs in the iron industry certainly occurred before the advent of the iron road and those that occurred later cannot be linked with railways *alone.* Fogel correctly observed that: 'metallurgical innovators could, have been and were lured to search for improved products and processes by the profit that was to be earned from sales in all markets for iron not just in the railroad market'. Fishlow seems more convinced that technical advance in *steel* could be systematically linked with railroads. To him, 'it comes as no surprise that Kelly's experimentation with the Bessemer process took place at the Cambria works, a substantial producer of rails or the Trenton works pioneered in structural beams'. The issue is not likely to be resolved, because economics does not propound a generally accepted theory of technical progress. In so far as neo-classical writing favours a demand theory of invention all new economic historians will accept the point that sales to railways constituted part of the environment that stimulated research into new technology for basic metallurgy.

Technological progress is not, however, a major focus of debate and economics does offer more satisfactory explanations for the diffusion of known technology among firms in the iron and steel industry. Here Fishlow claimed a positive role for railroads. Their demands, he wrote:

> contributed heavily to the important transition from charcoal to anthracite and ultimately to coke pig. Without a mineral fuel basis the industry could never have grown to the heights it soon reached. The first experimentation with anthracite did precede the railroad age, but it is also true that rail mills could utilise anthracite more efficiently than other users and that much of the consumption took place there. The ultimate lead of anthracite pig in 1855 and the widening margin thereafter was assured by continuing increases in rail production during the decade. Secondly, within the more restrictive, but important field of rolling, railroads achieved still greater pre-eminence than in their demands for pig iron. In 1860, rails constituted in volume more than 40 per cent of all rolled iron. Rail mills were the largest in the country and in the technological van.

For Britain Hawke could see 'no technological change' in rolling 'before 1870 that can be traced to demand for rails', but Fogel also admitted 'it is possible that technological innovations in the rolling of rails may have affected the technology of other rolling activities in the United States' but insists that the 'significance of such technological leadership is still to be established'. Similar quotations could be reproduced to show that historians of the French, Italian and German iron and steel industries see demand from railways as hastening the diffusion of more efficient technology

among European producers. But precise specification and measurement
of that effect remains elusive.

Demand from the construction and operation of railways may also
have raised the production of ferrous metals to levels where firms
found it possible to exploit economies of scale. Modern evidence
certainly shows that many sectors of the iron and steel industry are
subject to increasing returns over wide ranges of output. Fogel recognised the theoretical possibility that 'small changes in the demand for
iron due to rail consumption may either stimulate the growth of the
iron industry, leave it unaffected or retard it' and adds: 'which of
these alternatives applies to the American iron industry of the mid-
nineteenth century is an empirical question. The answer requires
data not now available'. He also argued, however, that: 'the demand
for iron by industries other than railroads was more than adequate to
permit a firm size capable of realising economies of scale in the production of non-railroad iron that were actually achieved prior to
1860.' Fishlow thought demand from railroads had promoted economies of scale in rail mills in the 1850s.

Both economists would agree that, in terms of the kind of investigations that are now undertaken on capacity utilisation and plant
size at different levels of output, the potential impetus to economies
of scale that emanated from railroad demand has not been adequately
investigated for the period 1840-1900. But *if* that demand led to an
earlier exploitation of economies of scale which resulted in cheaper
iron and steel for the economy at large, measurement of the benefits
from railways must include the full range of effects that flowed from
cheaper metals. Hawke made this point and agreed that demand for
rails played some part in shifting the demand curve for iron to a
level where it became profitable for smelters in South Wales to enlarge
the size of their blast furnaces. But to quantify or even to deny the
significance of increasing returns in the industry as a whole requires
evidence that is probably not available to the historians of the iron
industry.

Coming to steel: Fenoaltea shows how the Italian industry responded well to the unification of the domestic market as well as to the
direct purchases of steel by railways. Development in the British
steel industry lies beyond the period covered by Hawke's study. He
noticed that:

Hesitancy and rigid requirements for proof of the superiority
of steel on the part of railway companies implied that the use

of steel rails followed the development of the Bessemer steel
industry. The demand for steel rails may later have facilitated
the development of steel producers and possibly have made
available some economies of scale, but this did not occur
before 1870.

Development proceeded differently in the United States where 'after
the Civil war the Bessemer process was taken up first for the production of rails. Of the initial ten establishments fitted out for this purpose, seven were formerly iron rail mills'. Fogel is inclined to minimise the importance of economies of scale induced through the
impact of railroad demand on the size of Bessemer converters. This
diminution he achieved by expressing an ingenious calculation of
the gain from economies of scale in the steel industry as a share of
national income. Once again, the benefits will look rather small.
But historians of economic change normally focus attention on
the margin where benefits from innovations are perhaps better
expressed as a share of the increment to an industry's output over
some relevant time period.

Old economic history perceived that the progress of the iron and
steel industries in the nineteenth century could be explained — not
exclusively, not even overwhelmingly, but to an important degree —
in terms of the impact of demand generated by railways. That
cautious position has not been overturned by the new economic
history of railways and in fact is strengthened by Fishlow's investigation into backward linkages between railroads and the American
iron industry. Metallurgy, agreed, is just one industry which accounts
for a small share of value added by manufacturing as a whole and an
even smaller share of national output. But development theory assumes
that basic metallurgy is a type of industry that gives rise to externalities not captured by the usual measures of valued-added or physical
output. Thus further investigations into linkages between iron and
steel and other parts of the economy over relevant decades of the
nineteenth century are necessary for a full appraisal of the impact of
railroads.

Fogel and Hawke point out that the long-term growth of national
income, accompanied by rising levels of expenditure upon the output
of the iron and steel industry, would *in time* have produced nearly
all of the favourable linkages that accrued from railways. Demand
for metals is not a 'unique attribute' of the iron road. This is well
taken, but unless they can posit a plausible substitute for railway

demand such gains would presumably have accrued to society later
rather than earlier in the century. Lower levels of income and resources would probably impose cumulative reductions upon the
growth rate of national output. Impatient econometricians are sometimes apt to dismiss effects of this kind as 'lags'. Economic history
is about lags.

5 Railways and Other Industries

For other industries the new economic history of railways offers
nothing like the analysis and detail assembled for ferrous metals.
Hawke calculated that in the 1840s railways used about one third
of the output of Britain's brick fields. Perhaps their impact upon
the British coal industry also awaits attention because it can be
shown that by the 1860s railways absorbed a higher share of coal
output than any other single industry. Furthermore, in so far as
railways promoted urbanisation they stimulated demand for coal
as a domestic fuel. In America before the Civil War trains burned
wood rather than coal, but deliveries of coal as an input in metals
delivered to railroads raised overall demand 'direct and indirect to
about 5 per cent of the total output'. By the 1880s that ratio had
risen to nearly a fifth of output. Thus it is still plausible that when
the economic history of the coal and brick industries come to be
written, historians could find that demand from railways perhaps
helped to push those industries onto more efficient production
functions several years before any conceivable alternative source
of demand could have emerged to exert similar pressure. But as
Fogel ably demonstrated, for most other industries (except perhaps
for engineering) that possibility seems remote.

Engineering is interesting because of the range of its linkages with
other sectors. What part, then, did railways play in the development of a modern engineering industry and how did that development assist expansion elsewhere in the economy? Unfortunately,
until good monographs are published on European and American
engineering industries, new economic history could not fit railway
demand into context. Meanwhile the evidence it offered in the
studies on railways support some relevant points. For example,
Fishlow's conclusion that the *creation* of a machinery industry in
America owed little to demands for locomotives and other equipment
but can be 'explained by the existence of a prior level of skills and
technique upon which the industry could call' is perhaps even more

applicable to Britain but much less apposite for Russia and Italy. Nevertheless, it would be surprising to find that some of the solutions to technical problems posed by railways for metallurgy, thermo-dynamics and the manufacture of machine tools had no spin-offs to other parts of the engineering industry. Fogel argued thus about a whole range of inventions (including air brakes, block signals, car trucks, automatic coupling devices, track switches, pullman cars and equalising bars) which while they may have been important to the efficient operation of railroads . . . had no significant application outside of this industry during the nineteenth century'. But technical spin-offs are not exhausted by the adaptability of innovations to different users in the economy and Fogel could not examine the interconnections between different parts of the engineering industry. He also found only 6 per cent of engineering output was delivered to American railroads in 1859. Ratios of this kind may mislead historians trying to comprehend the process of growth. Engineering is a heterogenous industry and seems, in fact, more of a census than an analytical category. Thus for steam engines alone demands from railways in America in 1860 ranked second to shipping and Fishlow, interested in 'Railroads and the Transformation of the Ante Bellum economy' is less inclined to minimise the effects of railroads on the creation and 'geographic dissemination of skills necessary to an industrial society'. He perceived that:

> many railway repair shops were machine shops in miniature with their demands for lathes and other machine tools. While steamboats may have generated more power there were limited positive side effects for industrial development. And although the output of cotton and wool machinery exceeded locomotive production in 1860, the consequences were felt within narrow regional boundaries.

Hawke would agree in England that railway workshops were important centres for training engineers but concludes: 'Since this educational function did not require any characteristics peculiar to railways, it does not imply that dependence on railways was greater than the social saving indicated'.

But it is precisely such effects as spin-offs to the training of labour and management, the diffusion of skills and technology between and within industries, economies of scale and the whole learning process inherent in economic development that cannot be

captured within the conceptual folds of social saving — a conclusion that is more forcibly and eloquently made in the
contrasting approaches to American railroads found in the works
of Fishlow and Fogel.

6 FORWARD LINKAGES

1 Forward Linkages Specified

Railways not only provided the economy with cheaper inland transport they also compelled rival carriers (utilising ships and waggons) to lower their charges. In theory cheaper transport of all kinds conferred two general types of benefit upon the economy: firstly it released capital, labour and other resources for employment elsewhere in the productive system (these 'primary' benefits have already been analysed in discussion of social savings); secondly, railways brought markets and regions together, and this economic integration gave rise to external and internal economies which promoted greater efficiency and led to higher levels of production compared to the pre-railway situation. The benefits that flowed from the increased integration of markets brought about by railways (after referred to as forward linkages) are the subject of this chapter. A standard text-book diagram can be used to illustrate the

Diagram 2 Gains from Market Integration

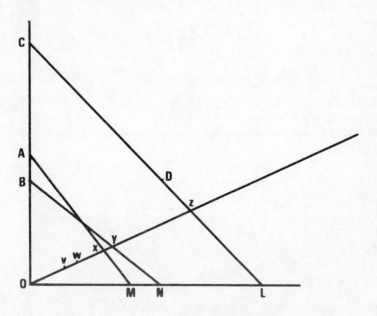

gains emanating from the increased trade and specialisation that followed from the increased integration of regions and markets by railways.

Stage 1 The Pre-Railway Age

Two regions north and south produce two commodities, corn and iron. AM is a production possibility curve representing the optimal combination of corn and iron that can be produced in the north with given factor supplies and techniques of production. BN is the production possibility curve for the south and represents potential production of combinations of corn and iron that can be produced in the south with its factor supplies and techniques of production.

Before the advent of railways demand and production and conditions led to an output of x of iron and textiles in the north and an output of y of iron and textiles in the south. Outputs x and y lie on a straight line indicating similar consumption patterns in the two regions.

Stage 2 The Advent of Railways

Railways integrate north and south with a single unit. Total consumption and production of iron and textiles will go up in the combined regions. This can be proved by summing the production possibility curves AM and BN in the diagram to give CDL (BC = OA, NL = OM). The co-ordinate of the integrated regions' consumption point z are greater than the sum of the co-ordinates x and y.

Thus since commodity substitution rates differed before the construction of railways and specialisation was incomplete, the integration of north and south within a single market raised real incomes and consumption compared to the pre-railway age.

The gains from the construction of railways will be even greater:

(1) If before integration misallocation of resources and underemployed labour characterised the economies of north and south. Illustrated on the diagram this would mean that production and consumption would not lie at x and y on the two production possibilities but to the left of these two points — say at w for the south and v for the north. The co-ordinates of the integrated regions' consumption point z is even more superior than the sum of the co-ordinates v and w.

(2) If integration stimulated competition so that resources were reallocated from less to more efficient firms or if firms moved from

less to more efficient locations similar gains will occur.

(3)   Where internal economies of scale in productive activities are present and the larger integrated markets created by railways enabled enterprises to realise these economies. This could be represented by an outward shift of the production possibility curves AM and BN after the construction of railways.

(4) The same effect would occur if markets enlarged by cheaper transport made possible the creation of new industries. Again the production possibility curves would shift to the right.

Through the mechanisms illustrated above cheaper transport helped to raise national incomes to the levels achieved by America, Britain and Russia over the second half of the nineteenth century. If data problems could be surmounted social savings could quantify the real costs of diverting freight from railways onto roads and waterways. Such estimates would then represent the costs to an economy of 'sustaining' the actual transport services provided by railways over any selected year. But while the extra costs of maintaining an equivalent transport service offers some measure of primary gain mentioned above, it does not include the benefits that accrued from access to additional natural resources nor does it measure the advantages derived from the more efficient location of agricultural and industrial activity. It does not quantify the gains that flowed from the reallocation of resources or the resources released by larger scale and improved forms of economic organisation that followed from the integration of markets.

Fogel introduced a fine distinction into this discussion which is a distinction between 'embodied' and 'disembodied' effects. Embodied benefits flow from the unique technical attributes of railroads and were obtained because substitutes for their services did not exist. If, for example, it can be shown that access to mineral deposits could *only* be achieved by rail, then the increment to the supply of minerals obtained constitutes a gain from railroads that is not included in calculations of social savings, which assumed that the closure of railways for one year would leave the level of output unchanged.

In retrospect 'unique technological attributes' are difficult to find. As Hawke and Fogel observed, access to land, minerals and more efficient locations rarely depend on railways. Hawke recognised, however, that 'railways opened up areas for coal mining that had not previously been used, and this process may have led to external economies in the north-east, in South Wales or in the inland coalfields'. Fogel is less inclined to look for resources rendered accessible by railroads even though minerals accounted in 1890 for over 50 per cent of their non-agricultural freight because he thought that 'a relatively small extension of the canal system could have brought most mines into direct contact with waterways' and 'very little supplementary waggon transport would have been required on these items'. Precise geological and engineering knowledge is required to measure 'embodied' effects of railroads and Fogel's critics are less certain that access to land and minerals could be provided by natural and artificial waterways, particularly when the frontier moved further westward after 1890.

Waterways apart, in engineering terms access is usually just as feasible by road as by railroad and the basic issue (as Fogel rightly insists) is one of costs not technology. Thus disembodied effects are usually far more important and would accrue from any form of cheap transport. Furthermore, in providing American and other economies with less expensive transport, railways did not initiate the decline in transport costs but simply carried forward a long process that probably achieved a decisive reduction in costs with artificial waterways. They 'reinforced tendencies' already underway before their introduction and diffusion. Thus the problem is to specify precisely where, when and to what extent railways offered producers critical reductions in transport charges which encouraged them to bring extra natural resources into production and to exploit economies of scale and location.

For Fogel, Metzer and Hawke social savings (based on actual flows of freight and national output for a given year) 'subsumes all of the disembodied effects of railroads' provided *'it is assumed that the existence of railroads did not alter the stock of resources'.* But social savings measures only the extra cost of carrying the actual flows of railroad freight on boats and waggons over one selected year towards the end of the diffusion of railways. *If* Americans, Englishmen or Russians had failed to construct railways some proportion of freight transported and national output for any selected year would simply not be there in 1865, 1890 or 1907. Fogel's distinction could be posited as an argument that something like the same positive effects on the long-term rate of growth would have been achieved if the American and Russian Governments had attracted aid from abroad and used money to subsidise transport by water and road so that charges per ton mile were equivalent to actual prices levied by railways. But in the real world it was cheaper transport offered by railways that year after year added to the flow of natural resources and influenced the location, specialisation and size of firms and farms in the direction of greater efficiency. Social savings does not separate out and measure the cumulative impact of these particular effects on the growth of national output. To reiterate a point made earlier, both the terminal quantities (ton miles) deployed to calculate social savings and the national product used as a denominator to express social savings as a ratio are not independent of the price and income effects on output and freight that emanated from the diffusion of railways over time. Social savings does not separate out and measure the benefits that would not have accrued if railways had not been constructed.

2   Railways and Natural Resources

For the United States (but not for settled countries such as Russia, Britain or Italy) the connection between extentions to the rail network and the supply of cultivable land are an important part of the process of economic development in the nineteenth century. For this relationship Fishlow's chapters on railroads and the transformation of agriculture in the ante-bellum economy represent a model combination of history and economics.

Fishlow first disposed of Schumpeter's hypothesis that railroads were built ahead of demand and thereby exerted an exogenous influence on the growth of national product. In fact he replaces Schumpeter's generalisation with the view that while investment in railroads responded to economic opportunities, capital and labour migrated to the frontier in 'anticipation' of future railroad construction: 'Thus subsequent development, although not initiated by the railroad is partially explained by its endogenous second round effects'.

Fishlow then takes up the impact of railroads upon the development of agriculture. First of all he qualified the orthodox view that their major effect was to open up land in the interior of America. He observed that up to 1860 other influences such as improved ploughs and drainage systems also helped to push the margin of cultivation further west. Furthermore, 'As commodity prices and land prices rose, those parts of the region formerly underutilised became relatively more attractive independently of transport innovation'. More significantly, Fishlow measured the share of the increment to grain output between 1850 and 1860 that emanated from areas that could be described as beyond the margin of cultivation before the extension of railroads. He defined such land as farms with below average yields and without access to waterways in 1849 and his statistics show that only a quarter of additional grain output came from such land. Thus the major contribution of railroads before the Civil War was to supply cheaper transport to existing centres of agricultural production and not to effect any *fundamental* shift in its location.

But this convincing analysis still left open the central question of the impact of the railroads upon agricultural output over the decade 1850-60. Their effects on production operated in two ways. Firstly in so far as they allowed farmers to move the margin of cultivation further west, railroads reduced the cost of land clearance, because land at the frontier could be reclaimed more cheaply than intra-marginal land. Secondly, virgin soil in the interior of America was more fecund than soil to the east and this free gift of nature implied that less labour and other agricultural inputs would be required per unit of output at the frontier. Fishlow estimated the gain from resources released from land reclamation at somewhere between $4.5 million and $9.0 million and the benefit from using soil of higher fecundity at about $14.9 million for 1859. He also hazarded a guess that if 'only 5 per cent of the increased supply of labour, capital and land in the West during the decade represented a response that would *not* have been forthcoming without the railroad' the product of Western agriculture would fall by $17.7 million. The sum of these gains amount to nearly $40 million, or around 3.6 per cent of agricultural output for 1859.

Fogel considered Fishlow to be in error when he added these gains to social savings, which already 'includes all of the increase in national income attributable to regional specialisation in agriculture induced by the decline in shipping costs'. In order to measure social savings, which is defined in a way which assumes that output and the pattern of freight shipments remain constant when the railroad is closed for one year, Fogel's comment is well taken. But Fishlow aimed basically to measure the effects upon agricultural production that actually emanated from the availability of cheaper transport provided by railroads over the decade 1850-60. For this particular historial exercise he was less concerned to ascertain the costs of closing down railroads for 1859 and focussed his analysis on answering the traditional question, namely the contribution of railroads to the growth of national income over time.

Fogel was also concerned with the relationship between railroads and the margin of cultivation in America, particularly when he attempted to estimate the decrease in the area of land cultivated that would follow from the closure of railroads in 1890. With great originality, he employed the theory of rent to locate a feasible frontier for commercial agriculture, which according to his calculations, outlined and criticised in Appendix 1, would lie approximately 40-50 miles from navigable waterways. Land beyond that boundary could not be cultivated (except on a subsistence basis) because the return on produce marketed would be less than the transport charges required to haul the surplus to market. Land beyond the boundary would go out of cultivation, unless served by the cheaper transport provided by railroads.

Both the methods and data Fogel employed to derive rental values for American farmland in 1890 have come under criticism from McClelland, while the conflation of average and marginal land values (a point developed in Appendix 1) imparts an upward bias to Fogel's estimate of the distance between his hypothetical agricultural frontier and navigable water. But really hard data is scarce and quantification is always useful. As Dr Johnson told Boswell, 'That, Sir, is the good of counting. It brings everything to a certainty which before floated in the mind indefinitely'. Fogel's ('controversial') figures imply that nearly a quarter of agricultural land (measured in value terms, not by area) would go out of cultivation if railroads had closed down in 1890. He goes on to argue that the American economy would, however, have adjusted to the absence of railroads by constructing an extra 5,000 miles of canals and improving public roads. His 'feasible' adjustments to the transport system would reduce the value of cultivable land in 1890 by a mere 4 per cent. The decline in area would, however, be much greater.

Very precise engineering knowledge is required to plan a canal and road system for an economy deprived of railways and Fogel's critics are not convinced that such knowledge was available to him. Moreover, as Wilson aptly remarked, 'I see no necessary reason to suppose that investors would have constructed 5,000 miles of canals if they had not constructed railways'. As they stand, Fogel's crude estimates do suggest that by 1890 something like a quarter of agricultural output might in fact be associated with extensions to the rail network. This contribution is not overwhelming but the influence of the railroad upon the availability of farmland certainly exceeded its effects for the period before the Civil War. But the precise reduction in the annual value of farmland or the level of agricultural output implied by a failure to build railways remains within very broad limits, indeterminate.

In an old economy like Britain the coming of railways probably had little effect upon the area of land cultivated but the innovation may have had greater impact upon the production of coal and other minerals. Again the problem is to ascertain whether critical reductions in transport costs provided producers with access to minerals that would have remained unexploited with canals and roads. Empirically such an effect seems impossible to measure. Hawke observed 'the siting of railways, especially in Yorkshire and the Midlands was influenced by potential coal traffic' and agreed with Mathews that 'railways enabled collieries to be established in areas of the North East previously untapped'. As for iron ore the period 1840-70 witnessed the growing importance of new fields such as Cleveland and the North West, but Hawke could not investigate the problem of whether deposits of coal and other minerals opened up after the construction of railways might have been 'economically accessible' by boat and waggon.

For Russian development White is convinced there was no feasible substitute for linking Donbas coking coal with Krivoi Rog iron ore deposits and 'the opportunity cost of the services provided by the Yekaterinin railway is, therefore, meaningless'.

By contrast both Fishlow and Fogel agree that most of America's mineral wealth could be readily exploited with the aid of water transport, which for bulky freight like coal and metallic ores offered a cheaper service per ton mile than railways. America's mineral wealth appears well located for transport by river or canal and its fortunate location implies a rather limited contribution from railroads. But precisely what that contribution amounted to over the nineteenth century has yet to be established.

3 Railways and the Location of Economic Activity

To what extent did the cheaper transport supplied by railways permit the American, British, Russian and other economies to reap benefits associated with regional specialisation and moves by firms to more efficient locations (equivalent to shifts of production possibility curves)? Such benefits are separable from the gains that producers derived directly from lower transport charges, and consist of the saving in real resources that the economy as a whole obtained from shifts towards optimal patterns of location.

Fogel recognised that without railways the spatial distribution of economic activity in America could have altered in a manner unfavourable to economic growth. But he is not inclined to rank that potential effect as important and makes the unverifiable assertion that 'many locations are consistent with the observed rate of growth'. Moreover, since Fogel's calculations revealed 'that in the absence of railroads extensions of canals and improvements in wagon roads would have kept in use all but 4 per cent of the land actually worked in 1890',

he also concludes 'such a limited reduction in the supply of land
leaves scant scope for alterations in the geographic locus of economic
activity'.

Fishlow's more detailed investigations support the conclusion
that railroads were not a necessary condition for the patterns of interregional trade and specialisation found in the United States before
the Civil War.   In his words:

> A basic conclusion following from this discussion of internal
> commerce is the limited contribution of the railroad before 1860
> in two of the three major axes of trade. Only in the flow between
> East and West and to a small degree in the opposite direction, did
> the trunk lines carry a large volume of traffic and even these with
> minor benefits.

Again it is the prior existence of roads and above all America's good
system of natural and artificial waterways that implied a small effect
from railroads in the creation and maintenance of interregional
trade. If such conclusions are true for the United States, with its
shifting frontier, they may be even more valid for more settled
economies like Britain and Italy and even for Russia. Hawke's view
that 'no large and dramatic changes in industrial location' can be
associated with railways will command assent.

Well specified research of this kind again helps to dispel exaggerated
claims for the impact of railways upon *broad* patterns of location. But
as Fishlow observed: 'Although the railroad patently did not create
interregional flows, it left a major imprint upon their direction and
magnitude even before 1860'. In other words the cheaper service
offered by railways had effects usually analysed in economics as gains
from trade creation and trade diversion. Fishlow did not measure such
gains but he investigated the kind of exports and imports carried by
rail in the trade between East and West before 1860 and shows the
importance of rail links to commodities like flour and livestock. He
also demonstrated how the rail linkages between the East and the
interior diverted trade from entrepôts like New Orleans. White and
Metzer both agreed that Russian railroads increased regional
specialisation and improved the allocation of resources in the production of rye and wheat, where according to White, 'There was a major
reorientation of resources towards those areas offering a higher
level of productivity'.

Interregional trade is, however, only the most obvious aspect of the problem. Associated with the spread of railways and lower transport charges there could be geographical shifts by enterprises within well defined economic regions that might result in external economies for society as a whole. Clearly, it was impossible to investigate this possibility as a by-product of research into the impact of railways. Until monographs are available on firms and industries that take up the matter of reductions in real costs that emanated from movements of firms between alternative locations, new economic historians can either bypass the question, or conduct a limited investigation, as did Fishlow, who looked into just two industries located in New England, namely textiles and boots and shoes. Alternatively they will find (as Hawke did) inadequate information in secondary literature on agricultural and industrial history. At present, benefits that accrued over the long run from the relocation of economic activity that followed from the introduction of railways cannot be properly investigated until the economic context for railways is more fully articulated.

4 Railways and Wider Markets

A similar agnostic conclusion seems to follow from investigations into the gains that come from wider markets. Here discussion is focussed upon the extension of *domestic* markets brought about by investment in railways. The new economic history did not analyse the benefits that the American, British, Russian or Italian economies derived from greater participation in the international economy, a participation associated with railways. A complete evaluation of social returns to British investment in railways should perhaps consider British capital invested in foreign as well as domestic railways. For the United States or Italy benefits from increased integration in the world economy that emanated specifically from their national rail networks were probably small.

But similar conclusions may be much less valid for Russia, and for that country White analysed the mechanisms through which railways stimulated the export of grain from 9 million cheverts in 1860-64 to 34 million cheverts by 1875-79 — exports which added about 4 per cent to national income and 'dwarfed the size of social savings calculated by conventional methods'. White admits, however, that although 'the export of grain on the scale actually achieved would have been very difficult in the absence of railways' it was 'perhaps possible with a major improvement to the canal systems leading to St.Petersburg'. But in his view railways exercised a 'unique' and it seems dramatic impact on Russian exports and output in several ways. Firstly they obviated the need to insure against local famine and part of the increment to exports came from 'grain . . . added to stocks and subsequently lost, stolen spoiled, or which had been consumed as liquor'. Railways promoted regional specialisation which also added to grain production with fixed inputs. The speedier movement of grain made it easier for Russians to derive advantage from price changes in the markets of Western Europe. Finally, the cheaper and more regular carriage of grain by rail enabled them to undercut their competitors from 'newer countries' when grain prices declined in the 1870s and 1880s.

When it comes to formulating the contribution of railways to the extension of *domestic* markets, Fogel's specification of the issue should be quoted in full. He warns:

It is erroneous to leap from data that demonstrates the victory of railroads over waterways in the competition for freight to the conclusion that the development of the railroad network was a prerequisite for the rapid continuous growth of the internal market. The only inference that can safely be drawn from such data is that railroads were providing transportation services at a cheaper cost to the buyer than other conveyances. For if rail transportation was a perfect or nearly perfect substitute for waterways, all that was required for a large shift from waterways to railroads was a small price differential in favour of the latter. Whether the shift produced a significant increase in the width of the internal market depends not on the volume of goods transferred from one medium to the other but on the magnitude of the associated reduction in transportation costs. If the reduction in costs achieved by railroads was small and if waterways could have all or most of the service that railroads were providing without increasing unit charges, then the presence of railroads did not substantially widen the market and their absence would not have kept it narrower. The conclusion that the railroad was a necessary condition for the widening the market thus flows not from a body of observed data but from the unverified assumption that the cost per unit of transportation was significantly less by rail than water.

We can agree that railways were not a necessary condition for the widening of domestic markets but the essence of the matter is not

charges by railroads compared to waterways but rather differences
in selling prices charged to consumers for commodities transported
to market by a combination of railways and waggons compared to
a second best solution of waggons and waterways. New economic
historians have demonstrated that reductions in total charges for the
transport of freight brought about by railways were not nearly so
dramatic as some historians imagined and were probably less
important than the decrease achieved by the shift of freight from
roads onto canals in an earlier period. Thus for Russia Metzer
emphasised, 'the crucial role of overland transport in generating
railroads' gains' because 'the pre-railway canal boom and . . .the
introduction of steamers . . . might have played a central role compared to which that of railways might have been only secondary'. And
he cited a preliminary calculation for Mexico by Coatsworth 'where
the only alternative to the railroads was overland transportation and
the rail social savings reached some 30 per cent of GNP'.

New economic historians are right to point out that no inference
can be drawn about the extension of the market from the superiority
of railroads over waterways, but unless the shape of demand curves
facing the producers of commodities transported to market by trains
are known it is also probable that little can be inferred from data
which simply shows percentage reductions in transport charges brought
about by investment in railways. Producers found it cheaper to send
freight on railways and indirectly the competition from the innovation
compelled carriers by road and water to lower their tariffs. Such
reductions were passed on to consumers in the form of lower commodity prices and the extent to which reduced commodity prices
widened the market depends upon the elasticity of demand for those
goods transferred from boats and waggons onto trains.

But are the benefits from larger markets not included in social
savings? David thought not, and argued that losses to an economy
from the closure of railways for one year do not include the gains
from extensions to the market associated with railways because
'introduction gains' could well be 'larger than withdrawal losses'.
For his objection to be valid two assumptions are required: (a) that
the long-run demand schedules facing producers in the nineteenth
century were price elastic; and (b) that their long-term marginal cost
curves were declining. On these two plausible premises the reduction
in transport charges brought about by railways would increase the
quantities of commodities sold and shift producers to lower points
on their long-term cost curves, where they realised increasing returns

to scale or higher levels of efficiency connected with the normal learning process. Such gains would not be reversed by the closure of railways for a single year. As David perceived:

> the indirect social gain attributable to the initial introduction of a transport innovation might very well exceed the full social loss occasioned by that innovation's subsequent withdrawal . . the proportional social burden of eventually losing access to a superior technique would be found to be quite limited because the indirect net benefits deriving from its previous utilisation had been, proportionately, far larger.

In other words, although social savings may answer a specific question on the costs of shutdown for year, it is not a substitute for an investigation into the gains realised over time from the introduction of an innovation. This is all too easily said and while the sequence of events that followed the introduction of railways can be described (as by older economic histories of transport) their impact upon extensions to the domestic market and through that upon the promotion of greater efficiency through competition and the reorganisation of enterprise into units closer to an optimal scale cannot be easily quantified.

For the United States Fogel did not pursue this kind of investigation but Fishlow's study contains two chapters on the effects of railroads before the Civil War. His conclusion diverges from Rostow's when he suggests that the prime beneficiary from wider markets associated with the spread of railroads was agriculture rather than industry. Perhaps Fishlow's conclusion should not surprise us, because agricultural produce is of lower value relative to weight than industrial commodities. Indeed he noticed: 'A ton of wheat sold for 30 dollars, a ton of cloth for 15 times as much'. Furthermore, American agricultural produce travelled further to market and the transport alternatives available to farmers involved more expensive haulage overland on poor roads than the alternatives available to industrialists.

Fishlow's thesis rests solidly upon a thorough survey of *all* the forces behind the upsurge of Eastern industry in the 1840s. In his work the railroad can be seen in context. For example, railroad construction in the East followed rather than preceded industrial expansion from 1840-47 and transport by water available for the

inputs and outputs of two of New England's major industries
(textiles and boots and shoes) implied a limited role for the railroad
in the extension of the market. Moreover he adds: 'in the 1850's,
with an expanding market due to better transportation of agricultural
products, manufacturers might have then received a positive stimulus.
But it did not come then because imports captured an increasing
share of the market.'

In the course of chapters designed to calculate social savings on
three commodities carried by railways (wheat, meat and minerals)
Hawke makes pertinent comments and presents useful statistics upon
their contribution to the extension of the market in England.
Apparently the agricultural interest had 'virtually unanimously
agreed . . . that it had considerably benefited from cheaper transport
charges which resulted from the building of railways'; but, Hawke
went on: 'this does raise the related problems of determining how
much agricultural produce was carried on railways, how great was
the saving in cost resulting from the availability of railways to carry
this produce and how important was this to the growth of the
economy'.

Accepting for the moment that wheat and meat are representative
of all agricultural produce marketed by rail, Hawke's estimate for the
quantity of domestic wheat so conveyed is a fine example of data
reconstruction. According to Hawke, in the mid-sixties, when wheat
occupied about half the acreage under grain, about 23½ million
bushels of wheat were transported by train between the surplus and
deficit counties of England. Unlike Fogel, Hawke made no attempt
to estimate the intraregional (or in this case, intra-country) tonnage
of wheat moved by rail and this could underestimate the shares of
the wheat surplus marked by railways.

While Hawke's figures are relevant and adequate for his objectives
it is difficult to calculate from them the kind of percentage reductions
in wheat prices in different markets throughout England that could
be associated with the construction of railways. But in a rough way
the exercise might be undertaken for London, which in 1865 consumed most of the wheat surplus produced in English counties. Accepting
Hawke's estimates that a surplus of nearly 19 million bushels of
English wheat moved by rail to supply London at a cost to shippers
of £322,000 then the transport element in the price of wheat
amounted to about 7 per cent of its selling price in the capital. But the
percentage required is not just the reduction in transport margins that
emanated from transferring wheat from waterways to railways but the

reduction in the level of wheat prices throughout the kingdom that
came also from the substitution of rail for road transport, where
the saving per ton mile was considerably greater. It is difficult to
appreciate whether the transfer of grain from road to rail was
important to the British economy, but there is no doubt of its
significance for Russia where, to quote White, 'many of the rail
links were built to compete with carting routes because of the great
cost savings involved. In these areas the possibility of water transport was non-existent'. And Metzer's estimate of social savings
for 1907 shows over 70 per cent of the total cost of transferring
freight from trains to waggons and waterways consisted of extra
charges for overland transport.

Finally, simple comparisons of transport charges for the movement of wheat by water or rail do not take account of possible
reductions in the price of grain that came about because railways
brought land further from the capital into competition with
adjacent counties. As quasi rents previously earned by factors
engaged in supplying London grain markets were forced downward
by the operation of market forces, over time, one would expect
some reallocation of land and other resources to a more efficient
mix of crops. Marginal farms would be compelled to improve their
methods. Resources would be reallocated from farms whose
comparative advantage lay not in wheat to farms who could produce
the grain more cheaply. But, in a nineteenth century context it
would not, perhaps, be realistic to anticipate much by way of gains
from economies of scale in wheat farming.

It seems clear that the impact of the railway on the production
of wheat can only be appreciated market by market and that
generalisations based upon routes well served by a pre-existing
system of waterways cannot be extrapolated to the rest of Britain.
As they stand, Hawke's figures which indicate that charges per
ton mile for conveying wheat by rail or water were not likely to be
very wide apart and certainly could be used for his basic purpose,
namely to warn us not to exaggerate the impact of the role of railways in widening the English market for domestic grain production,
particularly as the elasticity of demand for staple foodstuffs is not
normally high.

For livestock the same conclusion does not apply because costs
to farmers of sending cattle, sheep and pigs by rail were apparently
about half that by the alternative mode of marketing, namely droving.
(Animals seldom travelled by canal but where they could be sent to

market by sea the gap in transport margins disappeared.) Furthermore, demand for meat is usually more responsive to variations in retail prices than demand for wheat.

Without further research it is not possible to quantify the effects of the speed of railways upon British livestock farming or the indirect effects that flowed from the interrelationship between animal and arable farming. But Hawke's data takes us part of the way and he shows the majority of the 7 million sheep, nearly 2 million cattle and 1.4 million pigs carried to market by railways' companies in 1865 were retailed to consumers at prices reduced by a cut of around 50 per cent in the margin for transport, compared to droving. Just what this decrease was in percentage terms per pound of meat or what it implied for the development of animal farming is still not clear. Agricultural historians are disposed to regard it as important.

They also emphasise the significance of the *rapid* transit provided by railways for the extension of the trade in dead meat. Hawke's figures show that this development occurred in the latter decades of the nineteenth century, because in 1865 railways supplied only 5 to 7 million ton miles of services for the trade in dead meat compared to between 341 and 391 million ton miles for livestock carriage. Most dead meat travelled into London and the alternative cost of rapid conveyance by road exceeded the rates charged by railway companies by a multiple of about four. But what the growth of a trade in dead meat, closely associated with railways, implied for the long-term development of British agriculture also remains to be investigated and cannot be deduced from the measurement of social savings.

Coal and metallic ores are bulky and heavy in relation to value and thus the lower cost of carriage by rail could definitely widen the market for minerals. Hawke's chapter, designed to calculate social savings on mineral traffic for 1865, contains new information on the subject. For example, his data show that in 1865 railways supplied just over 2,000 million ton miles of transport for minerals. Three-quarters of that tonnage consisted of coal which travelled an average distance of 34 miles, mainly within coalfields and industrial areas. By 1865, although sea transport still competed with railways for the traffic in minerals, trains had captured most of the inland trade from canals.

Compared to artificial waterways English railways decreased freight costs by 70 per cent for coal and 64 per cent on other minerals. But where trains had replaced waggons cost reductions were far more dramatic. Hawke's estimates indicate average charges for minerals of 0.37d per ton mile by rail, 2.3d by canal and between 18d and 24d a ton mile by road. If railways had closed down in 1865 hauliers by road would have been called upon to supply supplementary cartage of 378 million ton miles for minerals. This is, however, only a small proportion of the services actually provided by railway companies for the carriage of coal and ores in 1865. Thus Hawke's figures do show the degree to which waterways in Britain could (unlike in Russia or Mexico) provide a viable alternative for railways without raising mineral prices by the kind of huge percentages implied by the substitution of waggons and carts for trains.

What the general level of mineral prices and output might have been without the cheaper transport supplied by railways need not be investigated as part of a social savings calculation. Some crude notion about prices can, however, be obtained by a brief consideration of deliveries from the Derbyshire coalfield to London in 1865, a year when that field provided 43 per cent of the capital's supply of coal. If Derbyshire coal sold (c.i.f.) for somewhere near the average price of coal marketed in the metropolis (namely 18s a ton) and assuming it could travel 125 miles by canal or rail (which is the distance from Derby to London), then transport costs would have gone up by 70 per cent and the wholesale price, without the cheaper haulage provided by railways, could have risen by 15 per cent.

Mineral prices also declined because railways brought regional coal fields into competition with one another for distant markets. Such effects are again difficult to document as a by-product of studies on transport but Hawke does mention the 'Vend' — the organisation of coal proprietors in the North-east which for generations had fixed prices and supplies of coal for the London market. With the spread of railways, other regions, particularly the Midlands, came into competition with the Northumberland and Durham coalfield for London and southern markets. The Vend then collapsed. Hawke argued that the integration of the market for coal associated with railways simply transferred income between producers in the North-east and London consumers. In the short run this may be the most obvious effect and hard evidence is difficult to find, but there seems to be no reason to derogate the predictions of micro theory on the impetus to efficiency provided by competition between regions and firms.

Forward linkages occurred when railway companies appeared as sellers of cheaper transport and widened markets for producers throughout an economy. Research on American and British railways demon-

strates a capacity for rigorous specification of the problem. While
Fishlow's study of interconnections between American railroads on
the one hand and Western agriculture, Eastern industrialisation and
patterns of domestic commerce on the other is revealing about the
complex mechanisms and processes that followed from the construction of railroads, Hawke's quantified warnings not to exaggerate the
impact of railways on the extension of markets in Britain — a small
country with integrated commodity markets adequately served by
water-borne transport into the major centres of population — are also
well taken. Nevertheless, the measurement of gains that actually
accrued to an economy from the extension of the market associated
with railways remains extremely difficult, a point exemplified in
more recent studies on Russian and Italian railways.

For Italy, Fenoaltea employed a macro model (with assumed
parameters for the propensities to consume, save and invest) to argue
that while the 'construction of peninsular trunk lines tended to unify
the domestic market' the only quantitatively significant forward
linkage 'appears to be on the production of ferrous metals'.
Apparently other industries were either already located close to their
markets or could not realise the potential for import substitution
achieved by ferrous metals. Fenoaltea's model is interesting, but his
conclusions rest upon assumed parameters and only a detailed
investigation industry by industry can really demonstrate the effects
upon firms and industries that flowed from the integration of the
Italian market.

For Russia, Metzer conducted a systematic investigation into the
relationship between railroad construction and the market for two
basic agricultural commodities, rye and wheat. To document the
improvement in interregional trade in these two crops that could be
associated with railways, he traced a systematic decline in the
differences between their prices in St Petersburg and Odessa from
1856 to 1859 and 1906 to 1910, a decline that accelerated after
1876-79. For the shorter period of 1893-1913 and with a far greater
range of price data available to him, Metzer calculated the secular
decline in price differentials for a dozen pairs of markets as well as
trends in the variances of price distributions for the same set of
markets. His carefully processed evidence for grain prices certainly
seems consistent with a conclusion that:

> the reduction in transportation costs associated with major
> railway construction had a decisive impact on the quality of

the interregional trade in European Russia. It played a major
role in improving interregional terms of trade as demonstrated
by the reduction in grain price differentials between regions.
About 83 per cent of the decline in price differentials could be
attributable to the railroad induced decline in transportation
costs.

Kelly's estimated trend coefficients of price differentials for petroleum
products for 1893-1912 in six pairs of cities is also consistent with
Metzer's results for rye and wheat. His criticism that Metzer did not
examine the sources of the reduction in transport charges by rail for
particular commodities is correct but pedantic. The reductions in
freight charges to producers came about in several ways: from the
construction of main lines between cities, from the construction of
branch lines, from improvements in the efficiency of railroads over
time and from decreases in State-controlled freight rates unmatched
by any change in the real cost of transhipment by rail. All these
mechanisms (subsumed in Metzer's paper under the umbrella term
'railroad construction') operated to diminish the margin of transport
charges embodied in the prices of commodities transhipped across
the regions of Russia.

Railway operation would seem to be a more appropriate term
than railroad construction. Nevertheless, Metzer's statistical
demonstration that railroads promoted the integration of the
Russian market between 1860 and 1913 remains convincing. Where
his paper is weak is in locating and measuring the gains in output
that flowed from the widening of the Russian market, associated
with railroads. He specified these gains clearly as an outward shift
in production possibilities in each region, a shift that emanated
from specialisation, economies of scale and interregional movements
in factors of production of the kind illustrated in Diagram 1.

White made similar claims for the operation of Russian railways:

In grain production there was a major reorientation of resources
towards those areas offering a higher level of productivity. There
is also evidence that in at least some cases the labour involved
would have been un- or underemployed without railways.

White went on to make quite substantial claims for the externalities
that could be associated with the spread of railways in Russia. In his
view they not only moved regional prices closer together but removed

'the most violent fluctuations in price' and reduced:

> the possibility of large windfall gains and losses for traders.
> The input of entrepreneurial risk-taking was thereby reduced.
> Secondly, agricultural producers also benefited from more
> secure conditions. Subsistence and semi-subsistence farmers,
> who were previously unprepared to risk exposure to the
> market, particularly in the purchase of basic foodstuffs,
> could now specialise with much less risk. The greater speed
> and regularity of movement created an environment favour-
> able to the application of rational business methods, etc.

Finally he contrasted the backward economy of the Russian type
with a dynamic economy (like America) 'in which the factors of
production are highly responsive to any new opportunity signalled
by price change' and where in his view 'it would hardly be surprising
to find that the social saving resulting from one specific innovation
was low'. Whereas in Russia railways 'stimulated competitive activity
and the mobility of factors of production and hastened the replacement of a subsistence by a market economy'.

Metzer calculated an indicator for the commercialisation of
agriculture, namely the share of the grain harvest shipped or marketed
by rail and waterway. This ratio increased from around 29 per cent
in 1878-85 to 42 per cent by 1906-10. But he argued, however, that
the lower level of economic development in Russia 'might have caused
a smaller use of transport services than the United States and thus
bring about a smaller impact of a given resource saving in the transport
sector on general economic activity'. He generalised 'that the application
of technological innovations in the infrastructure might have a greater
direct economic impact in an advanced economy than in a less developed one, which might not be able to realise their full benefits'.

The difficulties with these claims and counter-claims for the benefits
that accrued from the integration of markets by railways are not
matters of specification but are rather problems of quantification.
Economics can always help with specification and White's catalogue
of beneficial effects that flowed from the construction of Russian railways in the nineteenth century replicates the claims made for externalities associated with investment in social overhead capital in underdeveloped countries in the contemporary world.

Just how substantial they could be for poor countries today or
might have been for relatively backward economies in the nineteenth

century presents planners and historians with problems of measurement that seem equally impossible to surmount. For example, Metzer's attempt simply to chart the trend towards regional specialisation the production of wheat and rye is, as Hawke's note shows, inconsistent with the data he presented on the changes in the shares of wheat and rye output produced by different regions of Russia between 1870 and 1910. Presumably the only way to answer these questions is to study and where possible to measure the effects that railways actually had on the outputs and costs of firms, farms and industries in particular regions integrated into wider markets. Perhaps the forward linkages that undoubtedly flowed from the diffusion of railways cannot be appreciated as a by-product of the study of that innovation, still less from repeating theoretical possibilities that might emanate from investment in railways. There is no point in beginning debates that simply inflate or derogate the importance of externalities that came from railroads. Economists seem to have concluded that time alone will tell if claims for externalities associated with particular innovations materialise. For economic historians research alone will tell.

CONCLUSIONS

More than a decade ago trumpets heralded new economic history onto the academic stage. Today historians may prefer to appreciate its novelty in andante rather than allegro mood. Nevertheless success is manifold and even where results fall short of youthful promise, the attempts of new economic history to specify problems rigorously, to push forward the frontiers of quantification and to offer firmer conclusions about the causes of economic development are examples of intellectual endeavour which stretch the mind and excite the imagination.

This text is not a survey of new economic history but is concerned with what is perhaps its most famous contribution, that is with a body of research which tried to tackle a grand historical theme in a new manner and to say something definite about the relationship between railroads and economic growth in the nineteenth century. In their different ways, Fogel and Fishlow not only inspired research on the history of transport in economies outside America but gave rise to an important and continuing debate about method and the employment of economic theory in history.

Considerations of space as well as the comparative framework adopted here led to the omission of at least two important topics covered by Fishlow and Hawke. The first, passenger transport, is, however, fully discussed in two articles published recently. While the second topic, concerned with changes over time in factor productivity within the railroad industry itself, is best reviewed as part of a study on long-term production functions in economic history. There are other aspects of the history of railways neglected by new economic history itself. For example, connections between politics and railways (a link stressed in Fenoaltea's study of Italian railways); railways and urbanisation; railways and the mobility of labour; the finance of railways; the effects of railways on business organisation and the balance of payments to name but a few obvious subjects.

This book has been written around its central theme, namely the contribution that railways made to economic progress in the nineteenth century as suppliers of a technically more efficient service for the carriage of freight. And an attempt has been made to survey and to appraise the new economic history of railways in three contexts:

(a) as part of a debate on methodology in economic history;
(b) as contributions to a broader discussion of the role of transport
in economic development; (c) as history by juxtaposing the data
presented against the facts required to support the generalisations
now offered.

To begin with history, where tribute must be paid to the
substantial amounts of new statistical information generated by
all these studies, data related not merely to the transport sector
itself but also to industries supplying goods and services to railways.
My critique of statistical evidence is related almost entirely to the
figures used to support estimates of social savings and social rates
of return on investment in railways. Where it appears that the quality
of the information employed to estimate output for railways in the
real world, and for the output of substitute forms of transport for
railways in a counterfactual universe, seems satisfactory for the
United States in 1859 and for Russia in 1907, subject to some incon-
sistency for England and Wales in 1865, and different in kind for
America in 1890. Thus any evaluation of Fogel's figures in terms of
the usual canons applied to historical evidence may be beside the
point, because many of his estimates are explicitly presented as the
product of exercises in data reconstruction. He subtitled his book
'Essays in Economic History', and he demonstrates to good effect
how to employ economic theory to deduce proxies for data that are
either inaccessible or simply not available.

For Fogel's main purpose, which was to calculate social savings
as a percentage of America's national income for 1890 his rough
estimates suffice, but for an assessment of social rates of return on
investment in railroads or if we wished to compare their impact
upon the rate of growth with the effects of other innovations,
greater accuracy would be required. Where comparisons are involved,
there is reason to suspect from the comments of his critics that Fogel
made controversial assumptions in order to provide statistical back-
ing for tentative conclusions. Fogel is always clear and explicit about
his data. Unfortunately some of his assumptions, the employment
of samples with a narrow base and his impressionistic methods of
extrapolation tended to be lost sight of in the course of later
publications and Fogel's estimates came to be regarded as 'facts'
rather ingenious artifacts of theoretical constructs. New
economic historians make a point of revealing the potential direction

of bias in their figures, but a closer look at their basic calculations does not support the contention that such biases are uni-directional and not all the statistics presented can be accepted as upper or outer bound estimates.

Perhaps the most important doubt about the data presented in the new economic history of railways bears upon the non-representative character of the often tiny samples of rates per ton mile charged by railways companies and more particularly by hauliers along roads and waterways. Such scepticism will and should be reinforced by the controversy that surrounds the common assumption that these prices could, at the margin, serve as proxies for the social opportunity cost of factors of production employed in transport — in the real economies of America in 1859 and 1890, England in 1865, Russia in 1907, and, even more doubtfully, as 'real' costs in counterfactual economies deprived of the services of railways.

The statistics under review are used to formulate estimates of social savings — a conceptual innovation designed by Fogel and employed by Hawke and Metzer to sum up the significance of railways. Social savings (provided data problems could be overcome) would measure the additional costs inflicted upon an economy through the closure of its railway system for one year. But difficulty and controversy has arisen over the kind of inferences that can be drawn from such estimates for England, America and Russia.

For example, when social savings are expressed as a percentage of national income the benefits derived from the operation of railways appear small. The new transport system can no longer be regarded as indispensable or vital for the preservation of the levels of national income achieved by Britain in 1865, America in 1890 or Russia in 1907. Thus large claims made by Rostow and others for the importance of railways seem to be revealed as hyperbole.

But why should social savings be expressed as a percentage of gross national product when other ratios (based upon equally valid but smaller denominators) could be employed to make the shut-down of railways appear far more costly to the economy? In any case, is 5 per cent of GNP a large or a small number? Can the real significance of railways for economic growth be appreciated without reference to other innovations of comparable importance? Fogel concluded that 'compared to other advances in technology, the railroad certainly stands as one of the most important'. But a proper ranking of innovations in terms of social savings would require more accurate data than the statistics made available by these studies of British, American and Russian railways would allow. Furthermore, it is not at all clear how innovations could be ranked in any precise way without reference to the value of resources devoted to their development and diffusion across an economy or among firms in a given industry. In other words, historians interested in measuring the *relative* importance of an innovation would appear to be logically more secure if they calculated an average social rate of return upon the capital required for its diffusion and compared that rate with the rates of return obtained from investment in other innovations. Of course, the objections to the actual estimates presented by Fishlow and others which claim to measure social rates of return are well taken, but the criticism goes too far when it denies theoretical validity to historical or ex post facto cost benefit analysis. Whatever the difficulties, historians will surely persist in trying to study the allocation of resources by their forebears and will demand judgements which are, as far as possible, theoretically consistent and empirically based.

As they stand, and on their own, estimates of social savings for England, America or Russia appear to convey only limited information about the relative importance of railways compared to other innovations. Nor do calculations of social savings take us very far in quantifying the contribution of railways to the long-term transformation of the British, American or Russian economies in the nineteenth century. In dynamic terms their meaning seems ambiguous. Hawke insisted that such estimates simply measure the costs of 'sustaining' an economy without railways for one year, and nothing more. But the early publicity for new economic history did suggest it was after bigger game and that tigers rather than less regal beasts could be enmeshed in social savings.

In order to deal properly with Rostow's preoccupation (which was with the long-term impact of railways upon the economic development) there seems to be no substitute for a chronological treatment of backward and forward linkages from railways to the rest of the economy. But the new history is bounded in time: 1840-70 for England, 1861-1913 for Italy, 1870-1913 for Russia and 1840-60 and 1890 for the United States. It is no criticism, but it may be relevant to observe that these dates precluded a full investigation of connections between railways and the steel industry in both Britain and the United States. Backward linkages for such crucial decades as the 1870s and the 1880s in America still remain unexplored — even though the mileage of railroad track increased more than three times over those years (from 52,000 miles in 1869 to 182,000 miles in 1889). Perhaps the social savings framework adopted by Fogel, Hawke and others predisposed them to neglect chronology and to forego an analysis of backward linkages between railroads and the economy at interesting stages of that connection. In historical terms there may be little significance to terminal dates like 1865 for England, 1890 for the United States and 1907 for Russia. By contrast, the periods selected by Fishlow and Fenoaltea for the United States and Italy appear to be more self-contained and historiographically defensible for a study of railways and the transformation of an economy.

Such a minor quibble will not detract from the substantial contribution made by the studies under review to our knowledge of the connections between railways and economic growth. For example, we now appreciate that the construction of railways in England and the United States probably reduced cyclical instability. Opportunities to buy shares in railways companies possibly added to the volume of foreign funds available to the American, Italian and Russian economies. Railways may have increased rates of domestic savings through improvements to the institutions of domestic capital markets in Britain and America. But even notional quantification of these effects remains elusive.

By contrast, measurement of backward linkages between railways and industrialisation has certainly advanced. New statistics for the shares of ferrous metals, coal, engineering products, timber and bricks delivered to railways help to demolish the large claims made for the effects of demand from railroads on industrialisation in America and Italy and to place their demand for the output of British industry in proper perspective. New economic historians have also shown there is no evidence of any obvious or very close connections between investment in railways and technical progress in metallurgy or engineering.

A few well-made ratios can certainly be used with telling effect against notions that railways acted as a 'leading sector' in nineteenth century industrialisation — and perhaps also against the whole idea of 'unbalanced' growth, if that concept could be tightly defined. But measurement of the *relative* importance of railway demand in the growth process is far more difficult. Perhaps only a series of input-output tables could provide the data necessary to trace the full range of inter-connections between railways and industry over time. Meanwhile the importance of sales to railways for the development of ferrous metals, coal and the engineering industries is not settled and probably cannot be taken further until demand from railways can be fitted into studies on the long-term growth of those industries. In such a context it may be possible to comprehend the significance of purchases by railways over particular cycles of industrial expansion and contraction and to trace connections between that demand and the diffusion of improved technology and the realisation of economies of scale. On all these important subjects new economic history is rigorous in specification and makes original comments but hardly takes quantification more than one or two steps further.

Forward linkages, or the chain reactions that flowed from the availability of cheaper transport, also seem to elude and probably will continue to elude measurement. Railways carried forward the reduction in transport costs initiated by canals in the eighteenth century and thereby widened markets, stimulated competition and provided cheaper access to natural resources and to more efficient locations for productive activity. Historians wish to know; where, when and with what effect?

Fishlow's detailed historical analysis of the relationship between railroads and economic development over two decades issues in a well supported argument against exaggerating the contribution of railroads to economic progress in America before the Civil War. His work shows that transport by road and above all by water provided producers with easy access to land and other natural resources. Before 1860 American railroads were not built ahead of demand, did not open up very much of the interior to cultivation and added only a small proportion to the country's agricultural output. Furthermore, interregional trade and specialisation in America preceded the advent of the railroad, and trading patterns persisted after its early diffusion.

Between 1858 and 1889 the rail network expanded from 29,920 miles to 181,682 miles. Fogel's study was focussed upon 1890 and he devoted only limited space to the kind of questions that preoccupied Fishlow. His general position on forward linkages might be interpreted to imply that even in 1890 railroads made little difference to observed patterns of interregional trade or to the availability of natural resources. Internal trade and access to resources could, so Fogel argued, be serviced by a combination of boats and waggons at a higher but not a prohibitively higher cost to American producers. In other words, substitutes for railroads could *cope* with the transport required by America in 1890 without serious dislocation to economic activity. Fogel's conclusion leaves the actual (if small) contribution of the railroad to economic growth unresolved.

Since Adam Smith, economists and historians have dilated upon the beneficial effects that originated from extensions to the market. The mechanisms through which extensions associated with railways fed back to economic growth in the nineteenth century is rigorously stated by Hawke and Fogel, and the latter's point that nothing can be deduced about the widening of markets from the victory of railroads over canals is well taken. Fishlow documents and analyses the process over two decades before the Civil War and he shows that agriculture gained far more than Eastern industry from the integration of markets that came from cheaper transport and he describes the links between agricultural development and food processing industries in the ante-bellum economy.

By analysing trends in the differentials in regional grain prices, Metzer traced the process of market integration in Russia that came with railways between 1870 and 1907. But whether the integration of regional markets for agricultural commodities led on to the kind of shifts in production possibilities envisaged by White remains conjectural. Hawke's research into the transport of English wheat, minerals and meat in 1865 contains new and relevant data on the costs of hauling these commodities by rail compared to canal and road. For wheat his evidence suggests that the availability of rail transport made only a slight difference to its price in the London market. For minerals and meat (especially dead meat) the decline in (c.i.f.) prices brought about by the railways seem substantial. But precisely what these reductions in meat and mineral prices implied for the development of the agricultural and mining industries remains to be investigated.

To sum up: by 1914 railway lines radiated from all the great centres of industry in Western Europe and America. Almost everywhere agricultural and industrial growth accompanied the diffusion of this most dramatic of all nineteenth-century innovations and since their inception contemporaries and historians have never ceased to speculate about connections between railways and material progress over the second half of that century. New economic historians approached this grand historical theme equipped with the intellectual tool-kit of a post-Keynesian and post-computer generation. They came as Fishlow put it 'committed to quantitative techniques and to economics'.

The achievement is impressive. Their research on railways exemplifies all the virtues now recognised as the hallmarks of new economic history. Hypotheses are well specified and logically consistent; measurement is careful and sophisticated and substantial amounts of new data are generated by collection, collation and by way of imaginative inference based upon economic theory.

The broad conclusions of the new economic history of railways will surely endure and historians can no longer exaggerate the contribution of railways to economic development. Single innovations, even the accelerated growth of particular industries cannot now be described as leading an economy towards 'take off' or 'a drive to maturity'. Nineteenth-century growth is once again perceived as multi-factoral and complex; as a process in which no one input can be described as necessary or indispensable. Hyperbole and mono-causal explanations have certainly been checked.

Within the history of transport we now understand more clearly the mechanisms through which a decline in the cost of haulage saved real resources, widened markets, promoted local and regional specialisation and provided producers with access to natural resources. In all these ways railways carried forward a process that probably achieved a decisive breakthrough with canals. In fact one of the most interesting hypothesis thrown up by new economic history is that for Western Europe, Russia and the United States natural and artificial waterways probably made a greater contribution to long-term economic progress than their more publicised mechanical rival and that railways made their greatest contribution in substituting for overland transport.

In 1966 an enthusiastic review in *The Times Literary Supplement* hailed the new economic history which although 'less than ten years old' was 'already sweeping all before it'. It continued:

> Resting upon an alliance between mathematically sophisticated tools of measurement and the contribution of theoretical models, it promises a definitive solution to such problems as the economic efficiency of slavery or the contribution of railways to American economic growth.

To conclude that in the end new economic history has emphatically not offered a definitive solution to the impact of railways upon American, British, Russian or Italian economic growth in the nineteenth century is to reveal both the scope and the limitations of neo-classical economics and to point up those areas in history that defy quantification. History indeed remains 'a depressingly inexact science'. But to grapple with research of such quality and sophistication is to engage in serious methodological debate and to reach the intellectual frontiers of economic history.

APPENDIX 1 A SURVEY AND APPRAISAL
OF THE DATA

1 Data requirements 1: Ton Miles of Freight Transhipped before and after the Closure of Railways

This monograph is focussed mainly on the meaning and implications of attempts to define the *primary* benefits derived from railways in terms of the cost to an economy of their closure. But it is also necessary to deal in some detail with the formidable demands for data posed by calculations of social savings and to recognise differences in method and success among new economic historians in coping with the historian's perennial problem.

First and foremost they all required statistics of ton miles of freight carried by rail for the years selected. Secondly they needed estimates of the additional miles that the tonnage actually carried by trains would travel when reallocated onto boats and waggons. Ton miles of freight is an aggregate of the tonnage of different commodities carried by train multiplied by the distance travelled by each commodity. Unfortunately railway records do not supply the necessary figures and in every case the authors were compelled to construct their own estimates of data.

Fishlow seems to have the best data, largely because in 1856 the American Treasury collated a body of facts 'upon cost, capitalisation, revenues, interest payments and so forth for every railroad'. From this report Fishlow derived a structure of average rates per ton mile for freight carried by various railroads in 1855-56. For 1859 contemporary sources provided him with reasonable estimates of total receipts from commodities shipped by rail. Extrapolation of rates per ton mile for 1855 to 1859 supplied Fishlow with all the numbers required to calculate ton miles of freight carried by railroads for that particular year. He admitted, however, 'it is embarrassingly true that small absolute changes in rates yield substantial differences in final estimates of . . . ton miles'. The gap between his upper and lower bound estimates is 331 million ton miles of freight.

For Britain Hawke utilised official statistics of *tons* transported by train, but since he lacked information on the average distance traversed by this volume of freight, he frankly stated that 'ton mileage carried at any point of time cannot now be established with certainty'. His multiplier (or average distance travelled) of 33 miles was based upon a question put to a witness by an informed member of the Royal

Commission on Railways in 1865. These two numbers enabled Hawke to estimate the services performed by railways in England and Wales for 1865 at 3.1 billion ton miles of freight.

He also published evidence which can be used to cross check this estimate, because for three particular commodities, namely minerals, wheat and dead meat Hawke made separate calculations of the reduction in social costs effected by railways. Historians will recognise that the statistics Hawke presented for the ton miles of coal and other minerals, wheat and meat sent by rail are superior in quantity and quality to the evidence he used to measure ton miles for freight as a whole. But they may well be worried by the fact that Hawke's calculations of social savings on these three commodities (which in 1865 formed not more than 35 per cent of the total tonnage carried by trains) exceeded the social savings for freight as a whole by some £820,000, which is about 4 per cent of his original estimate for social saving of £14 million on total ton miles supplied by railways.

Thus Hawke's published figures suggest that all social saving came from the transport of minerals alone*. (This is in fact Hawke's own reconciliation of his macro and disaggregated measures of social saving.) Alternatively his critics might surmise that the macro estimate of 3.1 billion ton miles is too low and the probable source of understatement lies in the multiplier of 33 miles; sceptics might also hazard a guess that the rates Hawke used to calculate the monetary cost of shifting freight from railways onto ships and waggons are understated. Some combination of these two alternatives seems more likely than Hawke's own view that social saving (or the reduction in the volume of real resources employed by the transport sector) came *entirely* from the transport of minerals and especially from coal. This argument implies that for all other commodities, forming some 65 per cent of total freight tonnage, the direct effect of railways was simply to push down tariffs charged on waterways and roads and to transfer monopoly rents or monopoly profits from the owners of these alternative modes of transport to their users, without reducing inputs of capital, labour and other resources required to transport such freight between producers and consumers. Hawke may be correct when he suggests that the charges made by canals for the transport of minerals were lower, and presumably embodied a smaller element of rent, than the charges on other

---

*In a private communication Hawke wrote that there is 'partial information that can be used to confirm the reasonable nature of the 33 mile figure'. He also saw no reason to alter his view that social savings came from the transport of freight alone.

merchandise, but it seems difficult to believe that coal and other minerals were unique in this respect or that railways achieved reductions in real costs solely for the transport of minerals.

Metzer seems to have the best data on ton miles (pood-versts) of freight sent by rail in Tsarist Russia, culled from statistical year-books published by the Ministry of Ways and Communications. His only real data problem, as far as output is concerned, was to calculate the extra distance travelled by freight taken off the trains in the counterfactual case and placed on boats and waggons. His estimate is based upon a random sample of 25 routes (a 10 per cent sample of all trunk and short haul routes by rail). The distance that each commodity taken off the railroad would travel by water and road along these 25 routes was computed from official maps. But maps would presumably not reveal either whether the selected waterways were in fact navigable for each commodity, or whether the roads selected were passable for heavy and bulky freight such as coal and iron ore. These sceptical questions were probably answered in Metzer's thesis. But rather precise technical knowledge is required to redesign transport routes for commodities taken off trains in a country like Russia, where both terrain and climate form major obstacles to the transhipment of goods. Some of White's observations and economic geographies of Russia suggest that connections by rail were often the only feasible link between large parts of the territory and the roundabout nature of transport by waterways would possibly have added more miles than the average of 15 per cent calculated with sophistication by Metzer.

Fogel's estimates of ton miles of freight carried by American railroads are different in kind from those presented by Hawke and Fishlow. In the first place they relate to agricultural commodities and only by rough extrapolation to freight as a whole. Thus in Fogel's work freight refers to agricultural freight. Moreover, Fogel's estimates are, in general, not based upon collated records of railway companies, but more often upon his own ingenious reconstruction of the flows of produce from farms to consumers in 1890. In fact the reconstruction of data through the employment of economic theory is claimed by Fogel to be one of the hallmarks of new economic history and that characteristic is admirably displayed in his own book on railroads.

Fogel divided the American railroad system into two sectors: the first served interregional trade — that is trade from 11 major points of collection (or in his words 'primary markets') in the West to some 90 secondary markets in the East and South of the United States. Intraregional lines which linked 'well over 100 primary markets' with an unspecified number of rail shipment stations occupied the rest of the railroad system. According to Fogel's estimates, American railroads supplied services equivalent to 14.6 billion ton miles of freight in hauling agricultural commodities across regions and some 3.1 billion ton miles in shorter haulage within regions.

For interregional or long distance trade, Fogel made estimates for both tonnage and distance travelled by agricultural commodities in 1890. His estimates refer, however, to just four commodities: corn, wheat, beef and pork, which (he argued on the basis of value figures) dominated the trade. But the precise share of these four commodities to total output supplied by railroads for the transhipment of agricultural produce can only be determined with reference to total tonnage carried. Weight and distance conveyed rather than the value of cargo carried is the relevant indicator for railway output. Thus the importance of the sample remains indeterminate, but it is surely large enough for Fogel's purposes.

Fogel defined total tons of farm produce transported across the regions as equivalent to the demand for meat and grain in those parts of the United States where local supplies did not match local demand. While it is theoretically correct to define the marketed food surplus from agriculture as equivalent to quantity demanded plus exports and an adjustment for changes in stocks, ideally such an estimate should be built up on the basis of information related to family incomes and patterns of expenditure for families resident in the East and South — that is in those States that purchased the bulk of the American farm surplus in 1890. Perhaps the required data does not exist but the levels and distribution of incomes among the States of the Union was certainly not equal. Fogel based his estimate upon average or *per capita* consumption of pork, beef and wheat in physical units for the whole of America; a number which he then multiplied by the population resident within food deficit regions. From this crude proxy for total tons of meat and grain shipped regionally he deducted estimates of the quantities of grain and meat transported by *water* to arrive at the tonnage of grain and meat sent by rail over long distances. Only those more familiar with the data can competently assess the quality of the figures for tonnage actually shipped by water, but since the volume of rail freight is derived as a residual Fogel's final figure embodies all the errors of previous estimation. There is no obvious way of ascertaining the likely direction of bias. Its calculation turns upon prices, elasticities and differences in income.

Railroads provided more direct and shorter links between producers and consumers. This implied that the reallocation of freight to waterways and roads would raise the number of miles travelled by that freight, and for two reasons. Firstly, water routes were usually more circuitous. Secondly, distances between producers and rail shipment stations tended to be shorter than the distances between those same producers and the nearest shipment station on waterways. Thus the number of waggon miles demanded by producers increased when the economy was deprived of railways; not merely because waggons supplied a substitute for trains but because railway lines came closer to centres of production than the network of canals, rivers and sea routes. Miles (and therefore ton miles) of freight demanded from the transport system in the counterfactual economy will go up. Thus the second major fact required by all three authors was an estimate for the *extra* miles required to transport the same tonnage between the producers and consumers for an economy which suffered from the hypothetical closure of railways.

Hawke's figures carry conviction. His overall estimate is based upon a sample of rail miles actually travelled by 60 loads of *coal* (as described in a Royal Commission Report). With the aid of maps Hawke located and calculated that the additional water and waggon mileage required to make the journeys by canal amounted on average to 6 miles but with considerable dispersion about the mean.

Fishlow tackled the problem railroad by railroad, but the amount of hard information assembled is rather limited and, in the end, he simply extrapolated the extra miles required when freight was shifted off trains from scattered details related to a sample of trunk lines.

Fogel's calculations are again based upon his reconstruction of the distribution system. For interregional or long distance hauls he found that agricultural freight moved on average 926 miles by rail but when shifted onto boats would travel an extra 648 miles. He obtained this latter figure from a random sample of distances between 30 routes or pairs of cities by making the bold assumption that the number of miles (as the crow flies) between two points is equivalent to distance actually travelled by freight in 1890 between those same points. For the extra waggon mileage required to move farm produce to a relatively small number of secondary or final markets, not located on waterways, Fogel thought that such points were on average some 50 miles from navigable water.

But for intraregional trade Fogel departed radically from the methods employed by Fishlow and Hawke. For this sector of railway enterprise he recognised that the area of farmland cultivated in an economy deprived of railroads would diminish, and he also expected that the likely reaction of producers to the closure of railways would be to build more canals and to improve roads. Any inward shift of the agricultural frontier would, of course, reduce farm output and, *mutatis mutandis,* the marketed surplus transported from farms to consumers. But against this potential loss of output, Fogel's hypothetical extension to waterways and roads implied that the boundary for commercial agriculture would shift outwards again to a line somewhere between the actual agricultural frontier of 1890 and the frontier of an economy that suffered passively from the closure of railroads. Furthermore, within this 'counterfactual area' for commercial agriculture the number of extra miles demanded from hauliers along roads and waterways would be less than mileage implied in the kind of counterfactual economies posited by Metzer, Hawke and Fishlow, who, in their respective calculations, made no allowance for possible adjustments to the closure of railroads.

Logically, there is little to choose between relaxing or maintaining *ceteris paribus* assumptions. Fogel's version of the counterfactual allows producers time and potential to react to the absence of rail-roads and thus raises the whole issue of what is the plausible range of adjustments that could be predicted in such a counterfactual economy. Fogel concentrated, however, on measuring the ton miles of transport demanded within the 'new' frontier for agriculture — labelled in his words as the 'feasible region'.

His problems are certainly complex enough because his (perhaps more realistic) counterfactual exercise presupposes: (a) that it is possible to specify plausible extensions to the system of inland water-ways and improvements to roads that would have occurred had the American economy been deprived of railroads; (b) that the historian can locate the boundaries of the 'feasible region' for agriculture and quantify the decline in output implied by that boundary; and (c) that (within the new frontier) he can measure the extra distances travelled by freight between farms and primary markets on waggons and waterways compared to distance travelled by waggons and trains. More than one American historian regards Fogel's proposed extensions to internal water transportation (which includes 37 canals and feeders, some 5,000 miles in length) with scepticism. Gilbert Fite put his objection strongly; 'the maps showing navigable rivers and proposed canals are', he thought, 'preposterous', because 'some of the so-called rivers are mere streams that would hardly float a corn cob in high water'.

Apparently there is less scepticism about the proposed improvements to public roads. But since this part of the exercise only affects the final estimate of social saving by a very small amount the sceptics may well be quibbling.

Undoubtedly, the most important and difficult problem faced by Fogel was to define a hypothetical new frontier for American agriculture in 1890 and with brilliance and originality he brought the theory of rent to his aid. In theory land at the margin of cultivation is farmed at a rent equivalent to the *net* value of the produce marketed from that land. Land earning no rent over and above full costs of cultivation (which include normal rewards for labour and capital supplied by farmers and landowners) will not be cultivated. Net receipts from produce sold by farmers depends on the costs of transporting this produce to market. As transport charges decline net returns per acre increase and it becomes profitable to farm more land. Thus Fogel could define the margin of cultivation as a line which joins together all points on the map, where the net value of the surplus marketed by rail is just sufficient to pay the charges for transporting the produce of that land to market. In theoretical terms this satisfactorily defines and explains the boundary for feasible commercial agriculture. But can such a hypothetical line be drawn for America in 1890?

The figures required to do so include data on rents paid or imputed for the services of farmland, productivity per acre in physical units and charges per ton mile for the transport of agricultural commodities by boat and waggon. Fogel presented proxies for all these statistics in order 'to *say something* about the limits of the boundary of feasible commercial agriculture'. My criticism is not merely the rather obvious objection that his basic data refer to 23 rather untypical counties located in the North Atlantic region (a region with 99 per cent of its farmland located less than 40 miles from a navigable waterway; compared to 76 per cent for America as a whole). No, my objection is rather that Fogel's proxies are a substitution of average for marginal values and this introduces an upward bias into his estimate of the boundary for agriculture.

A summary of his calculations might make the exercise clearer. In 1890 the North Atlantic region contained nearly 63 million acres of farmland and its farmers shipped (according to Fogel's own rough estimates) nearly 6 million tons of produce to market by rail — that is an average 'surplus' of about 0.09 tons per acre. Fogel next used an official census to estimate the annual rental value of an average acre of farmland in the same region. McClelland's comments express

scepticism about the accuracy of the statistics of land values published
in the 11th Census as well as Fogel's manipulations of those statistics
in order to obtain an estimate of *pure* rent. But for purposes of
argument let us accept Fogel's figure of just under $1 as a representa-
tive average for rental value per acre. Let us also accept that the cost
of hauling the 'surplus' of 0.09 tons on waggons comes to 1.86 cents
per mile. It is then simply a matter of arithmetic to ascertain the
number of miles that this same surplus could be hauled before transport
charges equalled the annual rental value of land that produced it. Fully
adjusted, Fogel's calculations (i.e. rental values divided by 1.86 cents)
imply that the boundary for commercial agriculture (without railways)
would lie between '40-50 straight-line miles from a navigable waterway'

Briefly put, my objection is this: the annual value of farmland at
or near the boundary of cultivation is likely to be lower than land
within the frontier for cultivation. Fogel himself admits that land
closer to waterways tended to be much more productive. Furthermore,
it also seems likely that land near the margin of cultivation in 1890
marketed more tons per acre *by rail* than land closer to navigable
waterways. I wish to pose the possibility that as the agricultural
frontier shifted away from navigable waterways its rental value per
acre fell below the regional average and the share of produce sent to
market by train rose above the regional average. If this possibility
is admitted the employment of average instead of marginal values
could bias Fogel's estimate of 40 to 50 miles from waterways as the
boundary of feasible commercial agriculture in an upward direction.

To what it is difficult to determine, but a shift of just 10 miles
could mean a correction of up to 50 million dollars in the fall in
agricultural output implied by a shift in the margin of cultivation.
On the other hand, as the feasible region diminished in area extra
miles of waggon transport demanded by farmers would also decrease
because distances to waterways and the volume of farm produce
previously sent to market by rail would fall. To some extent this
would offset the upward bias of the boundary estimate, but again
it is not easy to determine by how much because it is difficult to
appraise the estimates of miles travelled by freight within the feasible
region, either on railroads or when reallocated onto waterways and
waggons.

For the extra waggon mileage demanded by farmers located within
the feasible region, Fogel recognised that he had to measure the
average distance between farms and waterways in the counterfactual
case ánd compare it with distances between these same farms and rail-

ways in 1890. If such averages could be obtained they would represent shipments of produce to market by nearly 4 million farmers. For the average mileage by road between farm and railway station Fogel used a survey conducted by the Department of Agriculture in 1906 which enquired into 'greatest distances of haul to railroad and steamboat shipping points'. This survey published figures of the average number of miles that waggons moved produce between farms and railroad stations, commodity by commodity. Fogel weighted these averages by his own estimates of tonnage shipped from farms across county boundaries in 1890.

For distances between farms and waterways in the feasible region Fogel used his estimate (that no farm could be profitably located less than 40 miles from a navigable waterway) to deduce that on average farmland was in fact located not less than 20 miles as the crow flies (or 28 miles by road) from canals or rivers.

The extra waggon miles travelled by freight in the feasible region deprived of railroads comes to 19 miles. But when he measured the additional waggon miles required per ton of agricultural freight out-side the redesigned frontier (assuming in other words that agriculture in the counterfactual economy did diminish in size) Fogel calculated that this economy required an additional 158 miles of waggon transport per ton of freight marketed. Either the railroads led to the substitution of trains for waggons on the massive scale implied by these numbers or there is something inconsistent here.

Turning finally to the estimates for the difference between miles of waterway and miles of rail travelled by produce en route from farms to primary markets, the methods and data employed to derive these estimates are not set out in detail. Fogel puts the average distance travel-led as freight moved between an unspecified number of rail shipment and an unknown number of primary markets at 115 miles and the distance that freight would have travelled by water in the counterfac-tual case at 81 miles. These figures refer, again, to a random sample of 23 counties in the North Atlantic region. Furthermore, we are told that 'distances from rail and water shipping points to primary markets were measured on maps'. Maps, to repeat a point made above, do not provide statistics of miles *actually* travelled by freight. They inform us about distances between two points. We are not fully informed about the total number of measured connections between shipment stations and primary markets; the type of average employed; nor offered any justification for the extrapolation of the measured average from what may be an unrepresentative sample to the entire intra-regional trade of the United States. Fogel admits that rail hauls were probably longer in the North Atlantic region than elsewhere in America and reveals that for the North Central region the miles that freight would travel by water compared to rail would be higher than the average distance measured in his preferred sample. This raises familiar questions about the possible range of dispersion about the average and the potential orders of magnitude and direction of error introduced by extrapolations of this kind.

In summary, to calculate the 'primary' benefits derived by an economy from railways three estimates expressed in physical units seem essential:

(a)   The actual ton miles of freight carried by railways

(b)   the additional ton miles of transport demanded by an economy deprived of railways

(c)   For Fogel's counterfactual economy, a measure of the loss of farm output due to changes in the margin of cultivation.

Sources now available do not provide historians with such statistics and these monographs are concerned in large part to fill that gap. Metzer's data for Russia seems to be very good but he might write more to satisfy historians that the postulated routes travelled by freight taken off trains in the counterfactual economy are feasible?

Fishlow presents acceptable figures for ton miles of services provided to the American economy by railroads in 1859, but he devoted less attention to the derivation of estimates for the additional ton miles of water and waggon transport required in the counterfactual case. From official statistics Hawke also obtained good figures for tons carried by rail in England and Wales in 1865, but to persuade historians that the conversion of this tonnage into ton miles is satisfactory he needs to reconcile his macro and micro estimates. While Fogel's estimates deliberately based upon ingenious exercises (which employ economic theory in order to reconstruct the distribution network for agricultural produce alone) contain several unverified and incompletely supported assumptions related both to the tons actually shipped by rail in 1890 and above all to the extra miles of road and water transport required in his own distinctive counterfactual economy.

Furthermore, it should be re-emphasised in this appendix on data that Fogel's calculations refer to a sample of agricultural produce (corn, wheat, beef and pork) carried by railroads and only by extrapolation to freight as a whole. Ton miles of services supplied by railroads to the American economy in 1890 is a statistic that is not securely established. Furthermore, even the ratio of Fogel's commodity sample to ton miles of transport supplied to the agricultural sector is uncertain. Corn, wheat, beef and pork formed 90 per cent of the tonnage carried on trains engaged in the *interregional* trade in farm produce and they accounted for 42 per cent of net value added in agriculture. The size of this sample of four commodities compared to ton miles supplied for inter- and intra- regional trade in all agricultural commodities also remains to be established.

Fogel put the gains derived by the American economy from the cheaper services that railroads supplied to agriculture at $214 million for 1890. He extrapolated this benefit to freight as a whole in two steps.

Firstly, he argued that the true social savings on agricultural freight should be reduced by $74 million because the extra capital costs incurred to transport freight by waterways and waggons in the counter-factual economy should be spread over all commodities transported by rail, and not imputed (as they were in his initial calculation) to agricultural commodities alone. Fishlow, 'granting the validity of the concern' feels 'the gesture is rather magnanimous' and is inclined to 'an allowance of closer to $30 million'.

Secondly, Fogel suggested 'that one can obtain a reasonable estimate of the social savings in the transportation of all freight by multiplying the combined inter- and intra-regional figures by four'. The suggestion is rationalised on the ground that 'agricultural products probably accounted for about one-fourth of the ton miles of transpor-tation services provided by railroads in 1890'. No hard evidence is provided to support this multiplier. Fishlow argued it is too low. Fishlow accepts Fogel's estimate of 36.8 million *tons* of agricultural commodities transported by train and assumed 'that the average haul for agricultural produce bore the same relationship to the overall average in 1890 as in 1932' — a year when official figures for average hauls by commodity are first available. On the basis of this plausible assumption, Fishlow calculated that the haul for agricultural produce came to 362 miles for 1890 and the share in ton mileage for freight as a whole he estimated to be closer to 17 per cent than Fogel's 25 per cent.

The third step in Fogel's extrapolation involved an assumption that the additional costs of transporting agricultural produce to market by boat and waggon in the counterfactual economy compared to the actual cost by train would be equal to or more than the extra costs for all other commodities. Fogel observed that the differential benefits different commodities obtained from railroads depended upon the availability of substitutes and the extra inventory and storage charges required to compensate for the absence of the safer, more regular and faster form of transport by rail. Since about half of non-agricultural *tonnage* carried on trains consisted of coal and other minerals, and given the availability of waterways for the transport of minerals, and given the rather low storage and inventory charges for coal, iron and other ores, Fogel is disposed to argue that the saving per ton mile on agricultural produce probably exceeded the saving per ton mile on other commodities. In other words, estimates of social saving derived by interpolation from agricultural produce are likely to be biased in an upward direction.

Again, Fishlow is sceptical because 'the agricultural benefits as they stand reflect the heavy weight of interregional transport in the total, representing two thirds of agricultural ton mileage at a marginal saving of scarcely more than one half cent per ton mile'. 'It seems doubtful that an average weighted so heavily by a type of transport where alternatives were readily available is relevant to all freight'. Fishlow's caution is justified because even if Fogel's argument about minerals is accepted, agricultural produce plus minerals (on his own figures) account for only 62½ per cent of ton miles supplied by rail-roads in 1890. Fishlow's revisions of Fogel's extrapolation raised social saving 'beyond ten per cent of income rather than falling well below 5'. Fogel seems disinclined to accept amendments to his original estimate because in a later publication he adopted a different method of extrapolation, based upon Fishlow's data for 1860. According to Fogel, Fishlow's estimates 'reveal that in 1860 the social saving per ton mile on non-agricultural commodities was only 46 per cent of that for agricultural goods'. The application of this differential to the ton miles of non-agricultural freight supplied by railroads in 1890 reduced social saving on freight as a whole 'to about 3 per cent of gross national product'.

The upshot of this debate between Fishlow and Fogel underlines the latter's frank admission:

of course the social saving has been computed only for agricultural commodities. Ultimate conclusions regarding the significance of the primary effect of railroads must await the computation of the saving on non agricultural items [and] no firm estimate of the social saving on non-agricultural items can be obtained without the detailed, protracted research required.

If historians could be convinced that all errors and assumptions were probably biased in an upward direction it would be legitimate to regard the data presented as a basis for maximal or upper bound estimates of social savings, but as offered in these monographs these estimates might be over or understated and no historian scrutinising the evidence is likely to be convinced that all deviations from the facts are in one direction or that errors of estimation tend to cancel out and leave some rough approximation to reality.

2 Data Requirements 2: Monetary and 'Real' Costs for the Reallocation of Freight

Freight reallocated from railways onto roads and waterways would cost producers more to send to market for three reasons:
(a) the distance travelled by freight would lengthen;
(b) the average charges per ton mile by a combination of boat and waggon would be higher than by a combination of train and waggon;
(c) the greater speed, reliability, safety and regularity of railways provided producers with benefits that could not be matched by rival forms of transport .

I have already dealt at length with estimates for the additional mileage of transport services required in the counterfactual economy as freight was moved off the railways and I will now proceed to contrast the information required with the data presented to evaluate the extra costs to the economy produced by the hypothetical closure of railways.

Given acceptable estimates for ton miles of different commodities sent by rail and knowledge about the cheapest available substitute method of despatching that freight to identical destinations, the data required to construct a *preliminary* estimate of the extra charges paid by producers is a schedule of current tariffs per ton mile charged by enterprises engaged in the transport of goods by road and water.

It seems fair to observe that not one of these studies presented anything like sufficient information on tariffs charged by road and water transport which could pass any of the standard tests applied to representative samples of data or to averages derived from such samples. Understandably, charges per ton mile of shipping different commodities along roads were most difficult to find. Metzer, for example, employed a simple average of all rates quoted in a contemporary source of the costs for hauling construction materials by waggon to railway lines. Since road haulage in Russia made use of underemployed agricultural labour, animals and carts, and the supply of such services fluctuated seasonally, the problems of calculating a representative average rate for European Russia is formidable. Thus the limited range of data used by Metzer will elicit both sympathy for his difficulties and scepticism, particularly as most of the social saving from Russian railroads came from the substitution of trains for waggons.

This is, however, something of an irrelevant objection because even if a more acceptable range of information could be found for freight rates by water and road, more serious doubts about the relationship of the published tariffs for trains, waggons and boats to social costs would need to be allayed before they could be employed to measure social savings. But that point has already been discussed in Chapter 3.

BIBLIOGRAPHY

Andreano, R., (ed), *The New Economic History: Recent Papers on Methodology,* 1972

Aydelotte, W.O., *Quantification in History,* 1971

Bateman, F. and Weiss, T., 'Profitability in Southern Manufacturing: Estimates for 1860', *Explorations in Economic History,* July 1975

Blackwell, W.L., *The Beginnings of Russian Industrialisation,* 1968

Boyd, H.J. and Walton, G.M., 'The Social Savings from Nineteenth Century Rail Passenger Services', *Explorations in Economic History,* vol. 9, 1972

Chandler, A.D. and Salisbury, S., 'The Railroads and Innovations in Modern Business Administration', in B. Mazlish, (ed.), *The Railroad and the Space Program, An Exploration in Historical Analogy,* 1965

Coatsworth, J., 'Railroads Freight Social Savings in Mexico' — a paper presented to the Economic History Workshop at Chicago University and cited by Metzer in 'Railroads in Tsarist Russia' (see below).

Coelho, P., 'Comment on Railroad Social Saving in Nineteenth Century America', *American Economic Review,* March 1968

Cootner, P.H., 'The Economic Impact of the Railroad Innovation' in B. Mazlish, (ed.), *The Railroad and the Space Program, An Exploration in Historical Analogy,* 1965

David, P.A., 'Transport Innovation and Economic Growth: Professor Fogel On and Off the Rails', *Economic History Review,* December 1969

Davis, L.E., 'Professor Fogel and the New Economic History', *Economic History Review,* December 1966.

Davis, L.E., Easterlin, R. and Parker, W., *et al, American Economic Growth,* 1972

Desai, M., 'Some Issues in Econometric History', *Economic History Review,* April 1968

Dowie, J., 'As If or Not As If: The Economic Historian as Hamlet', *Australian Economic History Review,* March, 1967

Engerman, S.L., 'The Economic Impact of the Civil War', *Explorations in Entrepreneurial History,* Spring/Summer 1966

Fenoaltea, S., 'Railroads and Italian Industrial Growth, 1861-1913', *Explorations in Economic History,* Summer 1972

Fishlow, A., *American Railroads and the Transformation of the Ante-Bellum Economy,* 1965

Fishlow, A., 'Productivity and Technological Change in the Railroad Sector', *National Bureau of Economic Research Studies in Income and Wealth*, Vol. 30, 1966

Fishlow, A., and Fogel, R.W., 'Quantitative Economic History – an Interim Evaluation', *Journal of Economic History*, March 1971

Fite, G.C., 'Review of Railroads and American Economic Growth', *Agricultural History*, April 1966

Fogel, R.W., *The Union Pacific Railroad: A Case in Premature Enterprise*, 1960

Fogel, R.W., 'A Quantitative Approach to the Study of Railroads in American Economic Growth', *Journal of Economic History*, June 1962

Fogel, R.W., *Railroads and American Economic Growth*, 1964

Fogel, R.W., 'The Reunification of Economic History with Economic Theory', *American Economic Review*, May 1965

Fogel, R.W., 'Railroads as an Analogy to the Space Effort', *Economic Journal*, January 1966

Fogel, R.W., 'The New Economic History, its Findings and Methods'. *Economic History Review*, December 1966

Fogel, R.W., 'The Specification Problem in Economic History', *Journal of Economic History*, September 1967

Fogel, R.W., and Engerman, S., (eds.), *The Reinterpretation of American Economic History*, 1971

Goodrich, C., (ed.), *Canals and American Economic Development*, 1961

Gould, J.D., 'Hypothetical History', *Economic History Review*, August 1969

Gunderson, G., 'The Nature of Social Saving', *Economic History Review*, August 1970

Hacker, L.M., 'The New Revolution in Economic History', *Explorations in Economic History*, Spring 1966

Hawke, G.R., 'Mr Hunt's Study of the Fogel Thesis: A Comment', *History*, February 1968

Hawke, G.R., *Railways and Economic Growth in England and Wales, 1840-1870*, 1970

Hawke, G.R., 'Railway Passenger Traffic in 1865', in D. McCloskey, (ed.) *Essays on a Mature Economy*, 1971

Hawke, G.R., 'Note on *Some Economic Aspects of Railroad Development in Tsarist Russia* by J. Metzer', unpublished

Hughes, J.R.T., 'Fact and Theory in Economic History', *Explorations in Economic History*, Winter 1966

Hunt, E.H., 'Railroad Social Saving in Nineteenth Century America', *American Economic Review,* September 1967

Hunt, E.H., 'The New Economic History: Professor Fogel's Study of American Railways', *History,* February 1968

Jackman, W.T., *The Development of Transportation in Modern England,* 1962

Jenks, L.H., 'Railroads as an Economic Force in American Development', *Journal of Economic History,* May 1944

Kelly, W., 'Railroad Development and Market Integration in Tsarist Russia: Evidence on Oil Products and Grain'. *Journal of Economic History,* December 1976

Lebergott, S., 'United States Transport Advance and Economic Growth', *Journal of Economic History,* December 1966

Little, I.M.D., and Mirrlees, J.A., *Manual of Industrial Project Analysis,* 1969

Mathias, P., 'Review of Railways and Economic Growth in England and Wales', *English Historical Review,* July 1972

McClelland, P., 'Railroads, American Growth and the New Economic History', *Journal of Economic History,* March 1968

McClelland, P., 'Social Rates of Return on American Railroads in the Nineteenth Century', *Economic History Review,* August 1972

McClelland, P., *Causal Explanation and Model Building in History: Economics and the New Economic History,* 1975

McCloskey, D., 'Review of G. Hawke, *Railways and Economic Growth in England and Wales, Economic History Review,* August 1971

Mercer, L., 'Rates of Return for Land Grant Railroads: the Central Pacific System', *Journal of Economic History,* September 1970

Metzer, J., 'Some Economic Aspects of Railroad Development in Tsarist Russia', *Journal of Economic History,* March 1973

Metzer, J., 'Railroad Development and Market Integration: The Case of Tsarist Russia', *Journal of Economic History,* September 1974

Metzer, J., 'Railroad Development and Market Integration: A Rejoinder', *Journal of Economic History,* December 1976

Metzer, J., 'Railroads in Tsarist Russia: Direct Gains and Implications', *Explorations in Economic History,* January 1976

Mishan, E.J., *Cost Benefit Analysis, An Introduction,* 1971

Mitchell, B., 'The Coming of the Railway and United Kingdom Economic Growth', *Journal of Economic History,* September 1964

Murphy, G.S., 'On Counterfactual Propositions', *History and Theory,* vol. 9, 1969

Nerlove, M., 'Railroads and American Economic Growth', *Journal of*

Economic History, March 1966

North, D.C., 'The State of Economic History', *American Economic Review*, May 1965

North, D. and Thomas, R.P., *The Rise of the Western World*, 1973

Parker, W.N., 'From New to Old Economic History', *Journal of Economic History*, March 1971

Rostow, W.W., *The Stages of Economic Growth*, 2nd edn., 1971

Reed, M., (ed.), *Railways in the Victorian Economy*, 1969

Reed, M., *Investment in Railways in Britain*, 1975

Taylor, G.R., 'Review of Railroads and American Economic Growth', *American Economic Review*, September 1965

Taylor, G.R. and Ellsworth, L.F., (eds.), *Approaches to American Economic History*, 1971

Temin, P., 'In Pursuit of the Exact', *The Times Literary Supplement*, July 1966

Temin, P., (ed.), *New Economic History*, 1973

Thomas, K., 'New Ways in History', *The Times Literary Supplement*, April 1966

Thomas, R.P. and Shetler, D.D., 'Railroad Social Savings: Comment', *American Economic Review*, March 1968

Westwood, J., *A History of Russian Railways*, 1964

White, C.M., 'The Concept of Social Saving in Theory and Practice', *Economic History Review*, February 1976

Williamson, G., 'Review of Railroads and American Economic Growth', *Economic Development and Cultural Change*, October 1965

Wilson, C., 'Transport as a Factor in the History of Economic Development', *Journal of European Economic History*, Fall 1973

Woodman, H.D., 'Economic History and Economic Theory', *Journal of Interdisciplinary History*, Autumn 1972.

INDEX

Ames, E. 19
Ashton, T.S. 16

beef 30, 85, 86, 87, 104
Blackwell, W. 19
Bolino A.C. 26
bricks 59, 69
British climateric 19

Chandler, A. 59
coal 26, 59, 69, 79, 87, 99, 102, 103
Coatsworth J. 83
Cole, W.A. 28
competition 21
consumers surplus 40, 41, 42, 43
Cootner, P. 65
counterfactuals: definitions 23, 31,
    32; feedbacks 55

David, P.: externalities 50; social
    rate of return 40, 53-54, 83-84
Deane, P. 28

electricity 28
Engerman, S. 13, 15
engineering 69-71
England and Wales and Great Britain:
    estimate of social savings for
    25, 26, 29, 30, 95, 96; long run
    growth in 28; waterway transport
    46, 47; overland transport 46, 87,
    88; social rates of return 52
externalities 39, 41, 50, 53, 74,
    90-92

feedbacks 21, 39, 55, 59-69, 96, 97
Fenoaltea, S. railway investment 55-
    57; feedbacks 60; scale economies
    67; market widening 89
Fishlow, A.; estimates of social savings
    24, 26, 27, 35; social savings for
    one year 29, 30; definitions of
    social savings 31, 32, 34; counter
    factual 31; social rate of return 40-43,
    51; opportunity costs 44; water-
    way transport 46; overland trans-
    port 46; stocks 48, 49; insurance

49; externalities 50; railway in-
investment 55-57; foreign capital
58; feedbacks 59-64; technical
progress 65, 66; scale economies
67; engineering 69, 71; natural
resources 76, 77, 79; location 80,
81, 99; market widening 89, 98,
99; statistics 101, 105, 109
Fogel, R. social savings estimate 23,
26, 35; axiom of indispensability
27; slavery 13; social savings for
one year 39, 30; definition of
social savings 32, 33; estimates
of social savings 33; counterfactual 33, 34; technical progress 39,
65, 66; opportunity costs 44;
waterway transport 46, 98, 105,
106, 108; overland transport 46,
108; land rents 48, 106, 107,
stocks 48, 49; insurance 49;
externalities 51; feedbacks 59-
64; scale economies 67, 68;
engineering 69-71; land and
natural resources 74, 75, 77, 79;
location 79, 80, 98; market widening 82; statistics 94, 95, 103,
106, 109, 112; extrapolation
109-112
forward linkages 21, 39, 72-75

Gallman, R. 15
Goodrich, C. 26

Hacker, L. 30
Hartwell, M. 15
Hawke, G. estimate of social savings
25, 26; definition of social savings
28, 31, 32, 34; social savings for
one year 29, 30; counterfactual
31; social rate of return 40-43, 52,
53; waterway transport 46, 47;
externalities 50; railway investment and capital markets 55, 57,
58, 59; feedbacks 60-64; technical
progress 66, 67; scale economies
67; engineering 70, 71; natural
resources 78, 79; agriculture 85-
87, 99; coal 87-99; statistics 101-